THE SMITHS

COMPLETE CHORD SONGBOOK

THE SMITHS

COMPLETE CHORD SONGBOOK

EVERY SONG RECORDED BY THE SMITHS

EXCLUSIVELY DISTRIBUTED BY

PLAYING GUIDE
7

ACCEPT YOURSELF
8

ASK
14

ASLEEP
12

BACK TO THE OLD HOUSE
20

BARBARISM BEGINS AT HOME
22

BIGMOUTH STRIKES AGAIN
17

THE BOY WITH THE THORN IN HIS SIDE
24

CEMETERY GATES
27

DEATH AT ONE'S ELBOW
30

DEATH OF A DISCO DANCER
32

THE DRAIZE TRAIN
34

FRANKLY, MR SHANKLY
36

GIRL AFRAID
38

GIRLFRIEND IN A COMA
40

GOLDEN LIGHTS
42

HALF A PERSON
44

HAND IN GLOVE
46

HANDSOME DEVIL
49

THE HAND THAT ROCKS THE CRADLE
52

THE HEADMASTER RITUAL
55

HEAVEN KNOWS I'M MISERABLE NOW
58

HOW SOON IS NOW?
61

I DON'T OWE YOU ANYTHING
64

I KEEP MINE HIDDEN
66

I KNOW IT'S OVER
68

I STARTED SOMETHING I COULDN'T FINISH
74

I WANT THE ONE I CAN'T HAVE
71

I WON'T SHARE YOU
76

IS IT REALLY SO STRANGE?
78

JEANE
81

LAST NIGHT I DREAMT THAT SOMEBODY LOVED ME
84

LONDON
86

MEAT IS MURDER
88

MISERABLE LIE
92

MONEY CHANGES EVERYTHING
90

NEVER HAD NO ONE EVER
96

NOWHERE FAST
98

OSCILLATE WILDLY
95

PAINT A VULGAR PICTURE
100

PANIC
104

PLEASE, PLEASE, PLEASE,
LET ME GET WHAT I WANT
106

PRETTY GIRLS MAKE GRAVES
108

THE QUEEN IS DEAD
110

REEL AROUND THE FOUNTAIN
114

RUBBER RING
117

A RUSH AND A PUSH AND
THE LAND IS OURS
120

RUSHOLME RUFFIANS
122

SHAKESPEARE'S SISTER
126

SHEILA TAKE A BOW
128

SHOPLIFTERS OF THE WORLD UNITE
130

SOME GIRLS ARE BIGGER
THAN OTHERS
132

STILL ILL
134

STOP ME IF YOU THINK YOU'VE
HEARD THIS ONE BEFORE
136

STRETCH OUT AND WAIT
139

SUFFER LITTLE CHILDREN
142

SWEET AND TENDER HOOLIGAN
146

THAT JOKE ISN'T
FUNNY ANYMORE
149

THERE IS A LIGHT THAT
NEVER GOES OUT
152

THESE THINGS TAKE TIME
158

THIS CHARMING MAN
154

THIS NIGHT HAS OPENED MY EYES
156

UNHAPPY BIRTHDAY
164

UNLOVEABLE
161

VICAR IN A TUTU
166

WELL I WONDER
168

WHAT DIFFERENCE DOES IT MAKE?
170

WHAT SHE SAID
172

WILLIAM, IT WAS REALLY NOTHING
174

WONDERFUL WOMAN
176

WORK IS A FOUR LETTER WORD
178

YOU JUST HAVEN'T
EARNED IT YET, BABY
180

YOU'VE GOT EVERYTHING NOW
183

DISCOGRAPHY
187

Published by
Hal Leonard

Exclusive Distributors:

Hal Leonard
7777 West Bluemound Road, Milwaukee, WI 53213
Email: info@halleonard.com
Hal Leonard Europe Limited
42 Wigmore Street Marylebone, London, W1U 2 RY
Email: info@halleonardeurope.com
Hal Leonard Australia Pty. Ltd.
4 Lentara Court Cheltenham, Victoria, 9132 Australia
Email: info@halleonard.com.au

Order No. AM92011
ISBN 0-7119-4118-1

This book © Copyright 2005 Hal Leonard

Cover designed by Michael Bell Design.
Cover photograph courtesy of Stephen Wright/smithsphotos.com

For all works contained herein: Unauthorized copying, arranging, adapting, recording, Internet posting, public performance, or other distribution of the music in this publication is an infringement of copyright. Infringers are liable under the law.

Printed in EU.

www.halleonard.com

Relative Tuning

The guitar can be tuned with the aid of pitch pipes or dedicated electronic guitar tuners which are available through your local music dealer. If you do not have a tuning device, you can use relative tuning. Estimate the pitch of the 6th string as near as possible to E or at least a comfortable pitch (not too high, as you might break other strings in tuning up). Then, while checking the various positions on the diagram, place a finger from your left hand on the:

5th fret of the E or 6th string and **tune the open A** (or 5th string) to the note (A)

5th fret of the A or 5th string and **tune the open D** (or 4th string) to the note (D)

5th fret of the D or 4th string and **tune the open G** (or 3rd string) to the note (G)

4th fret of the G or 3rd string and **tune the open B** (or 2nd string) to the note (B)

5th fret of the B or 2nd string and **tune the open E** (or 1st string) to the note (E)

Reading Chord Boxes

Chord boxes are diagrams of the guitar neck viewed head upwards, face on as illustrated. The top horizontal line is the nut, unless a higher fret number is indicated, the others are the frets.

The vertical lines are the strings, starting from E (or 6th) on the left to E (or 1st) on the right.

The black dots indicate where to place your fingers.

Strings marked with an O are played open, not fretted. Strings marked with an X should not be played.

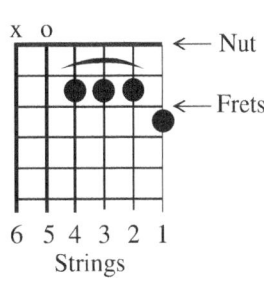

The curved bracket indicates a 'barre' - hold down the strings under the bracket with your first finger, using your other fingers to fret the remaining notes.

7

Accept Yourself

Words & Music by
Morrissey & Johnny Marr

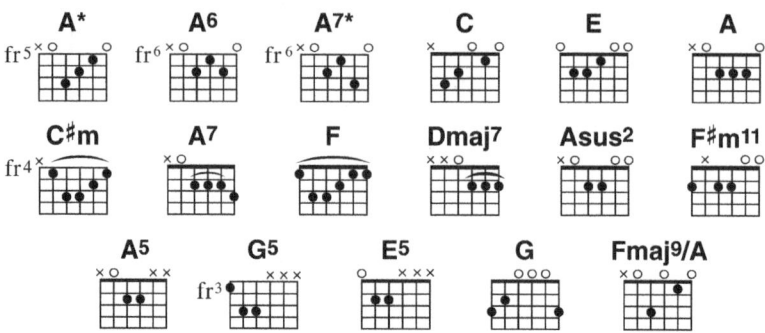

Capo third fret

	Riff 1		Riff 2	
Intro	|A* A6 A7* A6 | C E	|A* A6 A7* Asus4 | C E ||

Verse 1
    A   C#m
Everyday you must say,
  A7   F   E
"So how do I feel about my life?"
Riff 1   C   E   Riff 2
Anything is hard to find,
      C   E   A
When you will not open your eyes.
              C#m
When will you accept yourself?

    |A7 |F   E |C   E |

Bridge 1
Dmaj7 Asus2   F#m11 Dmaj7
I am sick and I am dull and I am plain,
                 Asus2   F#m11 Dmaj7
How dearly I'd love to get carried away.
                          Asus2   F#m11 Dmaj7
Oh but dreams have a knack of just not coming true,
        Asus2   F#m11   Dmaj7 E
And time is against me now.

Instrumental |A5 G5 |A5 E5 |A5 G5 |A5 E5 ||

© Copyright 1984 Marr Songs Limited/Artane Music Incorporated.
Chrysalis Music Limited (50%)/Universal Music Publishing Limited (50%).
All Rights Reserved. International Copyright Secured.

Verse 2

     Dmaj7   **Asus2**
      Who and what to blame?
Riff 1 **C**   **E**   **Riff 2**
    Anything is hard to find,
         C   **E**   **A**
When you will not open your eyes.
              C♯m
When will you accept yourself,
A7   **F**   **E**
   For Heaven's sake?
Riff 1 **C**   **E**   **Riff 2**
    Anything is hard to find,
         C   **E**   **A**
When you will not open your eyes.
      C♯m
Everyday   you must say,
A7   **F**   **E**   **F** **G**
  Oh how do I feel about the past?

Bridge 2

    Dmaj7   **Asus2**   **F♯m11** **Dmaj7**
    Others conquered love, but I ran,
                    Asus2   **F♯m11** **Dmaj7**
I sat in my room and I drew up a plan.
                               Asus2   **F♯m11** **Dmaj7**
Oh but plans can fall through as so often they do,
         Asus2   **F♯m11** **Dmaj7** **E**
And time is against me now.

Instrumental 2 As Instrumental 1

Verse 3

          Dmaj7   **Asus2**
And there's no-one left to blame
Riff 1   **C**   **E**   **Riff 2**
Oh_____ tell me when will you,
A   **C#m**
  When will you accept your life,
A7   **F**   **E**
  The one that you hate?
Riff 1 **C**   **E**   **Riff 2**
  For anything is hard to find,
          C   **E**   **A**
When you will not open your eyes.
               C#m
Everyday you must say,
A7   **F**   **E**   **F G**
  Oh how do I feel about my shoes?

Bridge 3

    Dmaj7   **Asus2**   **F#m11** **Dmaj7**
    They make me awkward and plain,
                      Asus2   **F#m11** **Dmaj7**
How dearly I would love to kick with the fray.
                        Asus2   **F#m11** **Dmaj7**
But I once had a dream and it never came true,
      Asus2
And time is against me now,
F#m11   **Dmaj7**   **E**
Time is against me now.

Instrumental 3 As Instrumental 1

Verse 4

              Dmaj7   **Asus2**
And there's no one but yourself to blame.
Riff 1   **C**   **E**   **Riff 2**
Oh____ anything is hard to find,
            C   **E**   **A**
When you will not open your eyes.
            C♯m
Anything is hard to find,
A7   **F**   **E**
   For Heaven's sake.
Riff 1   **C**   **E**   **Riff 2**
          Anything is hard to find,
           C   **E**   **A**
When you will not open your eyes.
             C♯m   **A7**
When will you accept yourself?
F   **E**   **F**   **G**
When?
F   **E**   **F**   **G**
When?
   F   **E**   **F**   **G**
Oh when?
F   **E**   **F**   **G** | **Fmaj9/A** ‖
When?

Asleep

Words & Music by
Morrissey & Johnny Marr

Chords: C Fmaj7 Am G Em/G D7sus2

Intro

| C | Fmaj7 | Am | Fmaj7 |

| G | ||

Verse 1

   C   Fmaj7
Sing me to sleep,
Am   Fmaj7
Sing me to sleep.
    G   Am
I'm tired and I,
  Fmaj7   G
I want to go to bed.
C   Fmaj7
Sing me to sleep,
Am   Fmaj7 G Am
Sing me to sleep,
    Fmaj7   G
And then leave me alone.

Verse 2

   C   Fmaj7   Am
Don't try to wake me in the morning,
  Fmaj7 G   Am Fmaj7
'Cos I will be gone.
G
  Don't feel bad for me,
      Fmaj7
I want you to know.
G
Deep in the cell of my heart,
    Fmaj7
I will feel so glad to go.

| Fmaj7 | Em/G | Fmaj7 | D7sus2 | Fmaj7 | Em/G ||

© Copyright 1985 Marr Songs Limited/Artane Music Incorporated.
Chrysalis Music Limited (50%)/Universal Music Publishing Limited (50%).
All Rights Reserved. International Copyright Secured.

Verse 3

|C   Fmaj7|
Sing me to sleep,
Am   Fmaj7
Sing me to sleep,
    G   Am   Fmaj7   G
I don't want to wake up on my own anymore.
C   Fmaj7
Sing to me,
Am   Fmaj7
Sing to me,
    G   Am   Fmaj7
I don't want to wake up on my own anymore.

Verse 4

G
   Don't feel bad for me,
     Fmaj7
I want you to know.
G
Deep in the cell of my heart,
    Fmaj7
I really want to go.
Fmaj7   Em/G   Fmaj7   D7sus2
   There is another world,
Fmaj7   Em/G
   There is a better world.
C   Fmaj7   Am
   Well, there must be,
Fmaj7   Am   Fmaj7
Well, there must be,
          C   Fmaj7 Am
Well, there must be,
Fmaj7   Am   Fmaj7
Well, there must be,
   G
Well…

Instrumental

Fmaj7	Fmaj7	Fmaj7	Fmaj7
G	G	G	G
Fmaj7	Fmaj7	Fmaj7	Fmaj7
Fmaj7	Em/G	Fmaj7	Em/G
Fmaj7	Em/G	Fmaj7	D7sus2 ‖

To fade

Ask

Words & Music by
Morrissey & Johnny Marr

G   Am7   C   D
C/G   Em7   Em7/D   Cmaj7

Intro | N.C. | N.C. | N.C. | G   Am7 | C   D ||

Verse 1
    G   Am7   C   D
Shyness is nice, and
  G   Am7   C   D
Shyness can stop you
    G   Am7   C   D   G   Am7   C   D
From doing all the things in life you'd like to.
  G   Am7   C   D
Shyness is nice, and
  G   Am7   C   D
Shyness can stop you
    G   Am7   C   D   G   Am7   C   D
From doing all the things in life you'd like to.
               G   Am7   C   D
So, if there's something you'd like to try
          G   Am7   C   D
If there's something you'd like to try
  G   Am7   C   D G   Am7   C   D
Ask me, I won't say "no", how could I?

© Copyright 1986 Marr Songs Limited/Artane Music Incorporated.
Chrysalis Music Limited (50%)/Universal Music Publishing Limited (50%).
All Rights Reserved. International Copyright Secured.

Verse 2

```
      G      Am7   C D
      Coyness is nice, and
      G      Am7   C    D
      Coyness can stop you
            G      Am7   C       D            G      Am7   C    D
      From saying all the things in life you'd like to
                G           Am7    C    D
      So, if there's something you'd like to try
              G          Am7    C    D
      If there's something you'd like to try
        G       Am7   C       D G   Am7  C    D
      Ask me, I won't say "no", how could I?
```

Bridge 1

```
              G    Am7     C D  G    Am7        C
      Spending warm Summer days indoors,
      D    G      Am7   C     D
      Writing frightening    verse
          G         Am7  C          D
      To a buck-toothed girl in Luxembourg.
```

Chorus 1

```
      G                         C/G
      Ask me, ask me, ask me,
      G
      Ask me, ask me, ask me,
              G  Am7   C
      Because  if it's not love,
          D     G        Am7      C          D
      Then it's the bomb, the bomb, the bomb, the bomb,
          G         Am7       C             D         (Em)
      The bomb, the bomb, the bomb that will bring us together.
```

| Em7 | Em7/D | Cmaj7 | Cmaj7 | |

| Em7 | Em7/D | C | C | ‖

Bridge 2

```
      G    Am7  C     D         G    Am7  C   D
      Nature  is a language, can't you read?
      G    Am7  C     D         G    Am7  C   D
      Nature  is a language, can't you read?
```

15

Chorus 2

```
        G                       C/G
Ask me, ask me, ask me,
G
Ask me, ask me, ask me,
        G      Am7     C
Because    if it's not love,
        D       G         Am7      C          D
Then it's the bomb, the bomb, the bomb, the bomb,
        G          Am7      C
The bomb, the bomb, the bomb
             D          G    Am7    C    D
That will bring us together.
G      Am7      C     D
   If it's not love
G         Am7     C    D
   Then it's the bomb,
G         Am7     C         D           G    Am7    C
   Then it's the bomb that will bring us together.
```

Coda

```
        D   G                  C/G
So    ask me, ask me, ask me,
G
Ask me, ask me, ask me.
```

```
||: G           | Am7          | C           | D           :||
                                        Repeat w/vocal ad lib. to fade
```

Bigmouth Strikes Again

Words & Music by
Morrissey & Johnny Marr

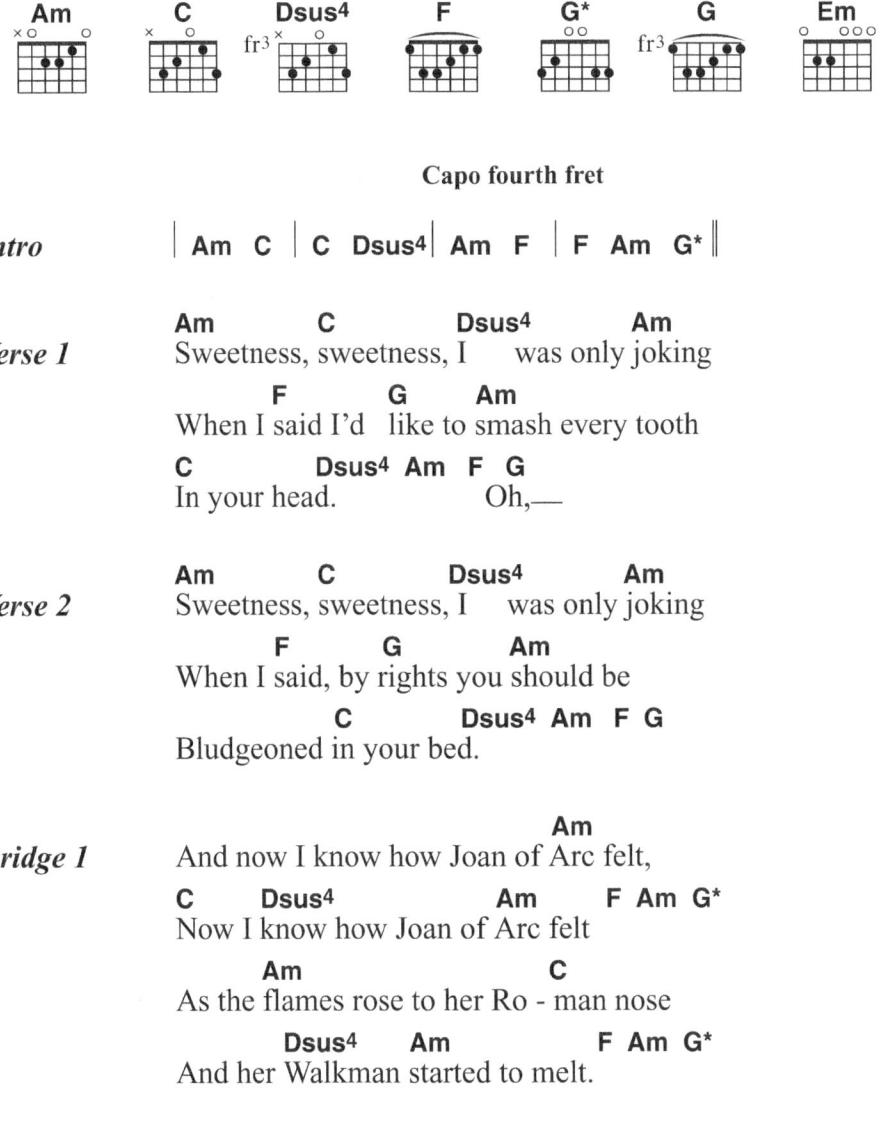

Capo fourth fret

Intro   ‖ Am C │ C Dsus4 Am F │ F Am G* ‖

Verse 1
       Am   C   Dsus4   Am
Sweetness, sweetness, I was only joking
      F   G   Am
When I said I'd like to smash every tooth
C   Dsus4 Am F G
In your head.   Oh,—

Verse 2
       Am   C   Dsus4   Am
Sweetness, sweetness, I was only joking
      F   G   Am
When I said, by rights you should be
         C   Dsus4 Am F G
Bludgeoned in your bed.

Bridge 1
                                Am
And now I know how Joan of Arc felt,
C   Dsus4   Am   F Am G*
Now I know how Joan of Arc felt
     Am   C
As the flames rose to her Ro - man nose
   Dsus4   Am   F Am G*
And her Walkman started to melt.

Instrumental 1 ‖: Am C │ C Dsus4 Am F │ F Am G :‖ *Play 4 times*

© Copyright 1986 Chrysalis Music Limited (50%)/Universal Music Publishing Limited (50%).
All Rights Reserved. International Copyright Secured.

Chorus 1

```
       Am          C Dsus4 Am           F
       Bigmouth, la,—      bigmouth, la.—
       G        Am
       Bigmouth strikes again,
                    C              Dsus4
       And I've got no right to take my place
                  Am        F G
       With the Human race.  Oh,—
       Am          C Dsus4 Am         F Am
       Bigmouth, la,—      bigmouth, la,
       G        Am
       Bigmouth strikes again,
                    C              Dsus4
       And I've got no right to take my place
                  Am        F G
       With the Human race.
```

Bridge 2

```
                                       Am
       And now I know how Joan of Arc felt,
       C       Dsus4          Am     F Am G*
       Now I know how Joan of Arc felt
            Am                  C
       As the flames rose to her Ro - man nose
              Dsus4     Am         F Am G*
       And her hearing aid   started to melt.
```

Instrumental 2 𝄆 Em | Em   D | Em | F G 𝄇

Chorus 2

```
       Am          C Dsus4 Am         F
       Bigmouth, la,—      bigmouth, la,—
       G        Am
       Bigmouth strikes again,
                    C              Dsus4
       And I've got no right to take my place
                 Am
       With the Human race.
       F Am G
       Oh...—
```

cont.

Am	C Dsus⁴	Am	F
Bigmouth, oh,— bigmouth, la,—

G   Am
Bigmouth strikes again,

     C   Dsus⁴
And I've got no right to take my place

    Am
With the Human race.

F G
Oh...—

Am   C Dsus⁴ Am   F
Bigmouth, oh,— bigmouth, la,—

G   Am
Bigmouth strikes again,

     C   Dsus⁴
And I've got no right to take my place

    Am
With the Human race.

F G
Oh...—

Am   C Dsus⁴ Am   F
Bigmouth, oh,— bigmouth, la,—

G   Am
Bigmouth strikes again,

     C   Dsus⁴
And I've got no right to take my place

    Am
With the Human race.

F G
Oh...— *To fade*

Back To The Old House

Words & Music by
Johnny Marr & Morrissey

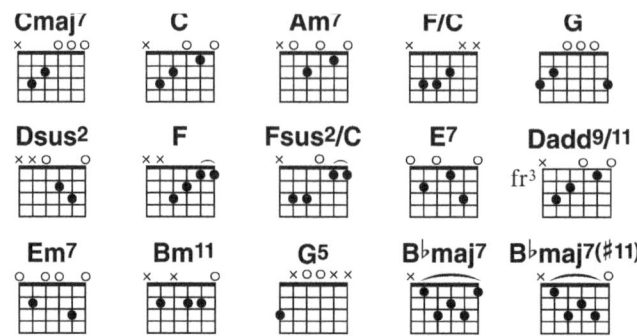

Capo second fret

Intro | Cmaj7 C | Am7 F/C G | Cmaj7 C | Am7 F/C G |
| Cmaj7 C | Am7 F/C G | Cmaj7 C | Dsus2 F/C G ||

Verse 1
      Cmaj7 C   Am7   F/C G
I would rather not go
Cmaj7 C   Am7   F/C G | Cmaj7 C   Am7   F/C G |
Back   to the old house.
Dsus2   F/C G   Cmaj7 C   Am7   F/C G
I   would rather not go
Cmaj7 C   Am7   F/C G
Back to the old house
F   G   Fsus2/C   G
    There's too many   bad   memories
Fsus2/C   G   E7   C   Dadd9/11
Too many   memories   there.

Instrumental 1 | Em7 | C   Dadd9/11 | Em7 | Bm11 |
| G5 | G5 | B♭maj7 | B♭maj7(#11) ||

Verse 2

  Cmaj7 C   Am7   F/C G
     When you cycled by,
  Cmaj7 C   Am7 F/C G
    Here began all my dreams,
  Cmaj7 C   Am7 F/C G C   Dsus2 F/C G
    The saddest thing I've ever seen.
  Cmaj7 C   Am7 F/C G
    And you never knew
    Cmaj7 C   Am7   F/C G
  How much I really liked you,
  Cmaj7 C   Am7 F/C G
    Because I never even told you,
  C   Dsus2 F/C G
   Oh, and I meant to.
  Cmaj7 C   Am7 F/C G Cmaj7 C
    Are you still there?
  F   G Fsus2/C G
   Or have you moved away?
  Fsus2/C G   E7 C   Dadd9/11
   Or have you moved away?

Instrumental 2 | Em7 | C   Dadd9/11 | Em7 | Bm11 |

      | G5 | G5 | B♭maj7 | B♭maj7(♯11) ||

Verse 3

    Cmaj7 C   Am7 F/C G
  I would love to go
  Cmaj7 C Am7 F/C G
  Back to the old house,
  Cmaj7 C Am7 F/C G
    But I never will,
  Cmaj7 C Am7 F/C G
    I never will,
  Cmaj7 C   Am7 F/C G Cmaj7 C Am7 F/C G
    I never   will,_____
  Cmaj7 C   Am7 F/C G Cmaj7 C Am7 F/C G
    I never   will,_____

Coda

  ||: Cmaj7 C | Am7 F/C G | Cmaj7 C | Am7 F/C G :||
                         Play 4 times
  🎵
  | Cmaj7 ||

Barbarism Begins At Home

Words & Music by
Morrissey & Johnny Marr

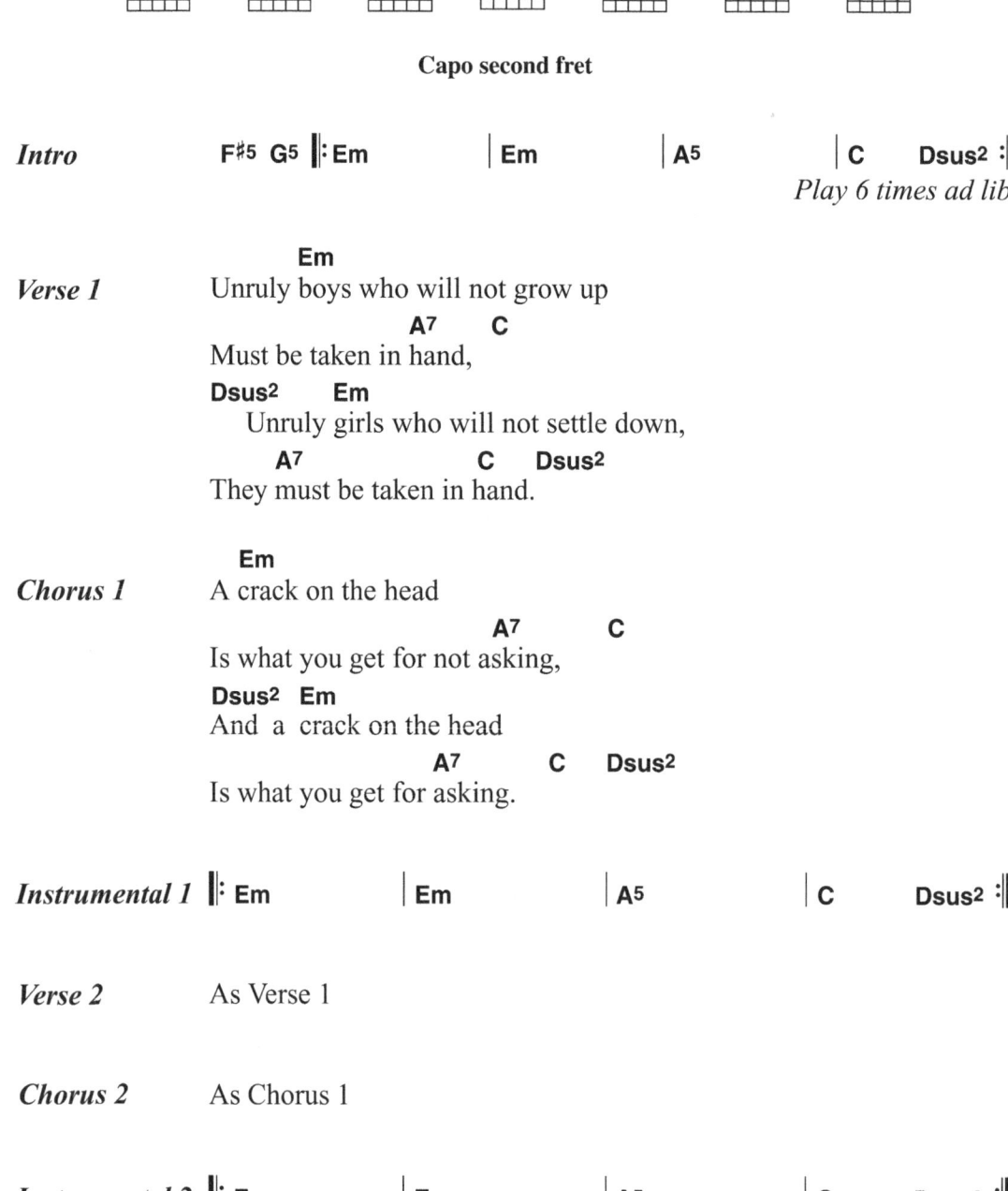

Chorus 3

      Em
No, a crack on the head
                     A7   C
Is what you get for not asking,
 Dsus2 Em
And a crack on the head
                 A7   C   Dsus2
Is what you get for asking.

Verse 3

           Em
A crack on the head

Is just what you get.
            A7   C
Why? Because of who you are!
 Dsus2   Em
A crack on the head

Is just what you get.
            A7   C
Why? Because of what you are!
 Dsus2   Em
A crack on the head
        A7   C   Dsus2 Em
Because of the things you   said,
           A7   C
Things you said, the things you did.

Verse 4

 Dsus2 Em
Un - ruly boys who will not grow
A7   C
Must be taken in hand,
 Dsus2 Em
Un - ruly girls who will not grow,
  A7   C   Dsus2
They must be taken in hand.

Coda

‖: Em | Em | A5 | C   Dsus2 :‖
Repeat ad lib. to fade

The Boy With The Thorn In His Side

Words & Music by
Morrissey & Johnny Marr

C   D   Dsus2   C*   G   Am7   Dsus4

Capo first fret
Tune slightly flat

Intro | C | | C D Dsus2 D | C | | C D Dsus2 D |

          | C | | C* | | Dsus4 | | Dsus2   D |

          | G | | G | ||

Verse 1
     D   Am7
The boy with the thorn in his side,
       C   D
Behind the hatred there lies
   G   D   Am7 C
A murderous desire   for love.
Dsus4 **D**   **Dsus2** **D** **G**   **D**
    How can   they look into my eyes,
                  Am7   C
And still they don't believe me?
Dsus4 **D**   **Dsus2** **D** **G**   **D**
    How can   they hear me say those words,
                  Am7   C
And still they don't believe me?
    Dsus4 **D**   **Dsus2** **D** **G**   **D**
And if   they   don't   believe me now,
        Am7   C
Will they ever believe me?
    Dsus4 **D**   **Dsus2** **D** **G**   **D**
And if   they   don't   believe me now,
                Am7
Will they ever, they ever believe me?
C   Dsus4 D   Dsus2   D
Oh, oh, oh.

© Copyright 1985 Marr Songs Limited/Artane Music Incorporated.
Chrysalis Music Limited (50%)/Universal Music Publishing Limited (50%).
All Rights Reserved. International Copyright Secured.

Instrumental 1 | C | | C D Dsus2 D | C | | C D Dsus2 D |
| C | | C* | | Dsus4 | | Dsus2 D |
| G | | G | | ‖

Verse 2

    D   Am7
The boy with the thorn in his side,
        C   D
Behind the hatred there lies
    G   D   Am7 C
A plundering desire   for love.
Dsus4 D   Dsus2 D G   D
       How can   they see the love in our eyes,
                    Am7
And still they don't believe us?
C   Dsus4 D   G
   And after all   this time,
D   Am7   C
  They don't want to believe us.
    Dsus4 D   Dsus2 D G   D
And if   they don't be - lieve us now,
    Am7   C
Will they ever believe us?
     Dsus4 D   Dsus2 D G
And when you want   to live,

How do you start?
D
Where do you go?
Am7
Who do you need to know?
C   Dsus4 D   Dsus2 D
Oh, oh, oh…

Instrumental 2 | C | C D Dsus² D | C | C D Dsus² D |
                   Oh…
                 | C | C* | Dsus⁴ | Dsus²   D |

                 | G | G   ‖

Instrumental 3 ‖: Dsus⁴ | Dsus⁴ D Dsus² D | Am⁷ | Am⁷ |

                 | C | C   D Dsus² D | G | G |

                 | Dsus⁴ | Dsus⁴ D Dsus² D | Am⁷ | Am⁷ |

                 | C | C   D Dsus² D | G | G   :‖
                                                                Repeat to fade

Cemetery Gates

Words & Music by
Morrissey & Johnny Marr

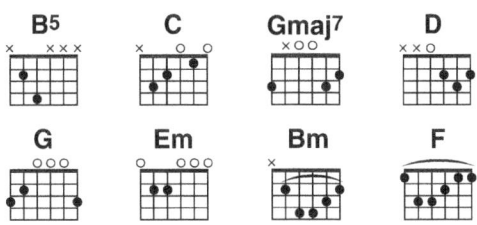

Intro   B5 | C   Gmaj7 | C   Gmaj7 | C | C   D   G ||

Verse 1
G
   A dreaded sunny day,
                         C
So I meet you at the cemetery gates,
           D   Em   C D
Keats and Yeats are on your side.
G
   A dreaded sunny day,
                         C
So I meet you at the cemetery gates,
           D   Em   C
Keats and Yeats are on your side,
        D   G
While Wi - lde is on mine.

Verse 2
G   C
     So we go inside and we gravely read the stones.
                    D
All those people all those lives,
             Em   C
Where are they now?
D   G
With their loves and hates,
                C
And passions just like mine,

They were born
            D   Em   C
And then they lived and then they died.
              D   G
Seems so unfair,   I want to cry.

© Copyright 1986 Marr Songs Limited/Artane Music Incorporated.
Chrysalis Music Limited (50%)/Universal Music Publishing Limited (50%).
All Rights Reserved. International Copyright Secured.

Bridge 1

                  Bm   Gmaj7
You say: "'Ere thrice the sun done salutation to the dawn,"
       Bm   Gmaj7
And you claim these words as your own,
     C   D
But I've read well, and I've heard them said
            Em   F
A hundred times, maybe less, maybe more.

Verse 3

      G
If you must write prose and poems
                        C
The words you use should be your own,
           D   Em
Don't plagiarise or take 'on loan.'
C   D   G
There's always someone, somewhere,
             C
With a big nose, who knows
            D   Em
And trips you up and laughs when you fall
C   D C   D   G
  Who'll trip you up and laugh when you fall.

Bridge 2

         Bm   Gmaj7
You say: "'Ere long done do does did,"
Bm   Gmaj7
Words which could only be your own.
    C
And then produce the text
   D
From whence was ripped
        Em   F
Some dizzy whore, eighteen hundred and four.

Verse 4

           G
A dreaded sunny day

So let's go where we're happy
                       C
And I meet you at the cemetery gates
         D   **Em**   **C**
Oh Keats and Yeats are on your side
  D   **G**
A dreaded sunny day

So let's go where we're wanted
                     C
And I meet you at the cemetery gates
     D   **Em**
Keats and Yeats are on your side
     C **D** **C** **D**   **G** **C G**
But you lose, 'cos Wil… Wilde is on mine.

Coda   ‖: C Gmaj7 | C Gmaj7 | C Gmaj7 | C Gmaj7 :‖

To fade

Death At One's Elbow

Words & Music by
Morrissey & Johnny Marr

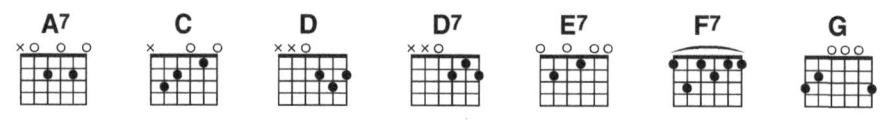

Intro ‖ Drums ‖

Verse 1
    A7   C   D   A7
Oh, Glenn, don't come to the house tonight.

Oh, Glenn,
      C   D   A7
Oh, Glenn, don't come to the house tonight,

Oh, Glenn,
     D7
Because there's somebody here
      A7
Who really really loves you. Oh, Glenn
  E7   F7   G
Stay home, be bored, it's crap, I know,
  A7
Tonight, oh, Glenn.

Verse 2
    A7   C   D   A7
Oh, Glenn, don't come to the house tonight.

Oh, Glenn,
      C   D   A7
Oh, Glenn, don't come to the house tonight,
     D7
Because there's somebody here
         A7
Who'll take a hatchet to your ear.
   E7   F7   G   A7
The frustration, it renders me hateful, Glenn!

© Copyright 1987 Marr Songs Limited/Artane Music Incorporated.
Chrysalis Music Limited (50%)/Universal Music Publishing Limited (50%).
All Rights Reserved. International Copyright Secured.

Verse 3

     A7   C   D   A7
        Don't come to the house tonight,
   C   D   A7
Don't come to the house tonight.
        D7   A7
Because you'll slip on the trail of all my sad remains,

That's why, that's why,
   E7   F7   G
Goodbye my love, goodbye my love,
   E7   F7   G
Goodbye my love, goodbye my love,

| A7 | A7 | |

   E7   F7   G
Goodbye my love, goodbye my love.

| A7 | ‖

Death Of A Disco Dancer

Words & Music by
Morrissey & Johnny Marr

|Intro| | B   B/A | G♯m7   Gmaj7 | B   B/A | G♯m7   E ||

Verse

     B   B/A   G♯m7 Gmaj7
The death of a disco dancer,
     B   B/A   G♯m7 E
Well, it happens a lot 'round here.
     B   B/A
And if you think peace is a common goal,
     G♯m7   Gmaj7   B   B/A G♯m7 E
That goes to show how little you know.
     B   B/A   G♯m7 Gmaj7
The death of a disco dancer,
     B   B/A   G♯m7 E
Well, I'd rather not get involved.
     B   B/A
I never talk to my neighbour,
     G♯m7   Gmaj7   B B/A G♯m7 E
I'd rather not get involved.

|Link| | B   B/A | G♯m7   Gmaj7 | B   B/A | G♯m7   E ||

Chorus 1

B   B/A   G♯m7   Gmaj7
Love, peace and harmony?
B   B/A   G♯m7 E
Love, peace and harmony?
     B   B/A
Oh, very nice, very nice,
     G♯m7   Gmaj7
Very nice, very nice,
               B   B/A G♯m7 E
…but maybe in the next world.

© Copyright 1987 Marr Songs Limited/Artane Music Incorporated.
Chrysalis Music Limited (50%)/Universal Music Publishing Limited (50%).
All Rights Reserved. International Copyright Secured.

Chorus 2

   B B/A   G♯m7 Gmaj7
Love, peace and harmony?
   B   B/A G♯m7 E
Love, peace and harmony?
   B   B/A
Oh, very nice, very nice,
    G♯m7   Gmaj7
Very nice, very nice, very nice,
        B
…but maybe in the next world,
       B/A
Maybe in the next world,
      G♯m7 E
Maybe in the next world.

Chorus 3 As Chorus 2 *ad lib.*

Coda   ‖: B B/A | G♯m7 Gmaj7 | B B/A | G♯m7 E :‖
                    Repeat w/vocal ad lib. to fade

The Draize Train

Words & Music by
Johnny Marr

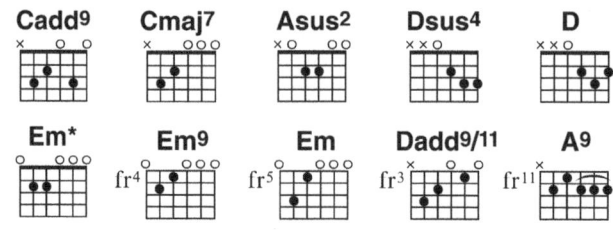

Intro		Cadd9		Cmaj7		Asus2		Dsus4 D	
		Em*		Em*		Em*		Em*	
		Cadd9		Cmaj7		Asus2		Dsus4 D	

"A1" ‖: Em Em9 Em | Em9 Em | Em Em9 Em | Em9 Em :‖
Play 8 times

"B1" ‖: Cadd9 | Cadd9 | Dadd9/11 | Dadd9/11 |
     | Em Em9 Em | Em9 Em | Em Em9 Em | Em9 Em :‖

"A2" ‖: Em Em9 Em | Em9 Em | Em Em9 Em | Em9 Em :‖
Play 4 times

"B2" ‖: Cadd9 | Cadd9 | Dadd9/11 | Dadd9/11 |
     | Em Em9 Em | Em9 Em | Em Em9 Em | Em9 Em :‖

"C1" ‖: A9 | A9 | A9 | A9 :‖
     | A9 | A9 | A9 | A9 |
     | Cadd9 | Cmaj7 | Asus2 | Dsus4 D ‖

"A3" ‖: Em Em9 Em | Em9 Em | Em Em9 Em | Em9 Em :‖
Play 4 times

© Copyright 1988 Marr Songs Limited.
Universal Music Publishing Limited.
All Rights Reserved. International Copyright Secured.

"B3"	‖: Cadd⁹	Cadd⁹	Dadd⁹/¹¹	Dadd⁹/¹¹	
	Em Em⁹ Em	Em⁹ Em	Em Em⁹ Em	Em⁹ Em :‖

"C2"	‖: A⁹	A⁹	A⁹	A⁹	
	A⁹	A⁹	A⁹	A⁹ :‖

"B4"	‖: Cadd⁹	Cadd⁹	Dadd⁹/¹¹	Dadd⁹/¹¹	
	Em Em⁹ Em	Em⁹ Em	Em Em⁹ Em	Em⁹ Em :‖

Play 11 times

Coda	Cadd⁹	Cadd⁹	Dadd⁹/¹¹	Dadd⁹/¹¹	
	Em* (fermata) ‖				

Frankly, Mr Shankly

**Words & Music by
Morrissey & Johnny Marr**

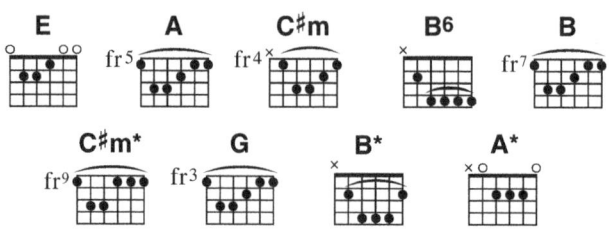

Intro | E ||

Verse 1
       A   C#m   B6
Frankly, Mr Shankly, this position I've held,
  C#m   B6   E
It pays my way and it corrodes my soul.
         A   C#m
I want to leave, you will not miss me,
B6   C#m   B6   A   E
   I want to go down in musical history.

Verse 2
   A   C#m   B6
Frankly, Mr Shankly, I'm a sickening wreck,
  C#m   B6   E
I've got the twenty-first century breathing down my neck.
         A   C#m
I must move fast, you understand me,
B6   C#m   B6   A
  I want to go down in celluloid history, Mr Shankly…

Instrumental | A E B C#m* | A E B C#m* | A E B C#m* | G   B E |

| A E B C#m* | A E B C#m* | A E B C#m* | G   B* A* |

| E ||

© Copyright 1986 Marr Songs Limited/Artane Music Incorporated.
Chrysalis Music Limited (50%)/Universal Music Publishing Limited (50%).
All Rights Reserved. International Copyright Secured.

Verse 3

```
        A              C#m     B6
Fame, fame, fatal fame,
          C#m      B6           E
It can play hideous tricks on the brain.
                  A
But still I'd rather be famous
        C#m        B6   C#m       B6     A        E
Than righteous or holy, any day, any day, any day.
```

Verse 4

```
          A                  C#m      B6
But sometimes I'd feel more fulfilled,
        C#m         B6             E
Making Christmas cards with the mentally ill.
              A            C#m     B6
I want to live and I want to love,
        C#m            B6         A            E
I want to catch something that I might be ashamed of.
```

Verse 5

```
A                    C#m           B6
Frankly, Mr Shankly, this position I've held,
  C#m      B6       E
It pays my way and it corrodes my soul.
                A               C#m      B6
Oh, I didn't realise that you wrote poetry,
        C#m              B6             A                E
I didn't realise you wrote such bloody awful poetry Mr Shankly.
```

Verse 6

```
A                            C#m     B6
Frankly, Mr Shankly, since you ask,
        C#m     B6      E
You are a flatulent pain the arse.
                A          C#m
I do not mean to be so rude,
  B6      C#m      B6     A
But still, I must speak frankly, Mr Shankly…
              E
Oh, give us yer money.
```

37

Girl Afraid

Words & Music by
Morrissey & Johnny Marr

Chords: Em, Bm, C, D, Am, D/G, Cmaj7, Bm7, Dmaj7, Gmaj7, C#m11, G#m7, Amaj7, Badd11, C#m7, E, Dsus2, Em*

Intro

Em Bm	C D
Em	Em	Am Bm	C D
|: Em	Em	Em	Em
Em	Em	D/G	Cmaj7 D :|
Em	Em	Am Bm	C D
Em	Em	Bm7	D Dmaj7
Em	Em	Am Bm	C D
Em	Em	

Verse 1

Bm7   D Dmaj7
   Girl afraid,
Bm7   D Dmaj7
Where do his intentions lay?
Gmaj7 C#m11   G#m7
Or does he even have any?
Amaj7 Badd11
   She said:
    C#m7   E   Amaj7
"He   never really looks at me,
Badd11   C#m7   E   Amaj7
   I give him every opportunity.

© Copyright 1984 Marr Songs Limited/Artane Music Incorporated.
Chrysalis Music Limited (50%)/Universal Music Publishing Limited (50%).
All Rights Reserved. International Copyright Secured.

Verse 1 (cont.)

    C♯m7   E
In the room downstairs,
    Amaj7   Badd11
He sat and stared.
    C♯m7   E
In the room downstairs,
      Amaj7
He sat and stared,
Badd11   Amaj7   Dsus2
    I'll never make that mistake again!"

Instrumental 1

Em	Em	Em	Em
D/G	Cmaj7 D	Em	Em
Em	Em	Em	Em
D/G	Cmaj7 D	Em	Em
Am Bm	C D	Em	Em
Bm7	D Dmaj7	Em	Em
Am Bm	C D	Em	Em	

Verse 2

Bm7   D Dmaj7
    Boy afraid,
Bm7   D Dmaj7
Prudence never pays,
  Gmaj7   C♯m11   G♯m7
And everything she wants costs money.
Amaj7 Badd11 C♯m7   E   Amaj7
  "But she   doesn't even like me!
Badd11   C♯m7   E   Amaj7
  And know because she said so,
Badd11   C♯m7   E
  In the room downstairs.
    Amaj7   Badd11
She sat and stared,
    C♯m7   E
In the room downstairs.
      Amaj7
She sat and stared,
Badd11   Amaj7   Dsus2   Em*
    I'll never make that mistake again! No."

Girlfriend In A Coma

Words & Music by
Morrissey & Johnny Marr

C   F   G   G*   Am   Am/G   F*

Capo seventh fret

Intro | C   F | C   F C | C   F | C   F C |
       | C   F | C   F C | C   F | C ||

Chorus 1
      C   G   F
Girlfriend in a coma, I know,
  G*   C G F G*
I know, it's serious.
C   G   F
Girlfriend in a coma, I know,
  G*   C G F G*
I know, it's really serious.

Verse 1
          C   G   F G* C   G
There were times when I could have murdered her,
 F   G*   C G F   G*
(But, you know, I would hate anything to happen to her.)
C G   F   G*
  No, I don't want to see her.
    Am   Am/G   F*
Do you really think   she'll pull through?
Am/G Am   Am/G F*   Am/G
Do you really think she'll pull   through?

| Am   Am/G | F*   G* |

Chorus 2

```
           C            G       F
Girlfriend in a coma, I know,
      G*     C    G   F  G*
I know. It's serious.
      C    G      F        G*       C    G    F   G*
My, my, my, my, my, my baby, goodbye.
```

Verse 2

```
                   C           G        F  G*   C
There were times when I could have strangled her,
     F          G*      C    G    F         G*
   (But, you know, I would hate anything to happen to her.)
 C  G          F          G*
      Would you please let me see her!
           Am         Am/G       F*
Do you really think    she'll pull through?
Am/G  Am              Am/G     F*     Am/G
Do you really think she'll pull    through?

| Am       Am/G | F*       G*    |
```

Coda

```
          C       G         F
Let me whisper my last goodbyes,
    G*        C
I know. It's serious.
```

41

Golden Lights

Words & Music by
Lynn Ripley

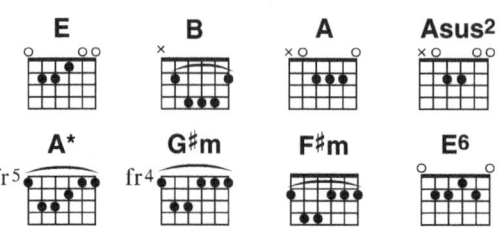

Intro

| E | ||

Chorus 1

```
     E                  B
Golden lights displaying your name,
     E                   B
Golden lights, it's a terrible shame.
       E      A
But oh, my darling,
     E   B      E      B
Why did you change?
```

Verse 1

```
     E                 B
Boy in a million, idol, a big star,
     E                  B
I didn't tell you how great you were.
 A
I didn't grovel and scream,
                                    B
Or rip your brand new jacket at the seams.
```

Verse 2

```
     E                      B
You made a record, they liked your singing,
     E                   B
All of a sudden the phone stops ringing,
 A
I never thought that you would let
                         B
The glory make you forget.
```

© Copyright 1987 Carlin Music Corporation.
All Rights Reserved. International Copyright Secured.

Chorus 2   As Chorus 1

Instrumental || E | A | E | B ||

Verse 3
    E   B
Top ten idol, king of your age,
    E   B
Who do you turn to when you're backstage?
A
Don't you remember, you once knew a girl,
                       B
You loved her more than the world?

Verse 4
    E   B
Is life always like this, brother?
    E   B
Good for one side, and bad for another.
A
I must put you behind me tonight,
               B
'Cos you belong to the lights.

Chorus 3
           E   B
There's golden lights displaying your name,
    E   B
Golden lights, it's a terrible shame.
     E   A
But oh, my darling,
E   B   E   B
Why did you change?
E   A
Oh, oh, my darling,
E   B   E   B
Why, why did you change?

Coda | Asus2 | A*   G♯m F♯m | E6 ||
                                                                                        To fade

Half A Person

Words & Music by
Morrissey & Johnny Marr

Chords: Gmaj7, E, Bm, Bm/A, G, A, F#m, F#, C

Intro | Gmaj7 | E ||

Verse 1
       Gmaj7   E
Call me morbid, call me pale,
       Gmaj7   E
I've spent six years on your trail,
Bm Bm/A G   E   A
Six long   years on your trail.
       Gmaj7   E
Call me morbid, call me pale,
       Gmaj7   E
I've spent six years on your trail,
Bm Bm/A   G   E   A
Six full years of my life on your trail.

Chorus 1
       F#m   F#   G   E A
And if you have five seconds to spare,
       F#m   F#   G   C G
Then I'll tell you the story of my life:
D   A
Sixteen, clumsy and shy,
F#   Bm G
  I went to London and I,
  D   A F#
I booked myself in at the Y… W.C.A.
       Gmaj7   E
I said, "I like it here. Can I stay?
       Gmaj7   E
I like it here. Can I stay?
Bm   Bm/A G   E   A
Do you have a vacancy for a back-scrubber?"

© Copyright 1987 Marr Songs Limited/Artane Music Incorporated.
Chrysalis Music Limited (50%)/Universal Music Publishing Limited (50%).
All Rights Reserved. International Copyright Secured.

Verse 2

    Gmaj7   E
She was left behind and sour,
    Gmaj7   E
And she wrote to me, equally dour.
        Bm   Bm/A   G
She said, "In the days when you were hopelessly poor,
    E   A
I just liked you more."

Chorus 2 As Chorus 1

Verse 3

    Gmaj7   E
Call me morbid, call me pale
    Gmaj7   E
I've spent too long on your trail
Bm Bm/A G   E A
Far too long chasing your tail, oh.

Chorus 3

     F#m   F#   G E A
And if you have five seconds to spare,
    F#m   F#   G C G
Then I'll tell you the story of my life:
D   A
Sixteen, clumsy and shy,
    F#   Bm G
That's the story of my life.
D   A
Sixteen, clumsy and shy,
  F#m   F#
The story of my life,

Coda

     Gmaj7   E
𝄆 That's the story of my life,
 Gmaj7   E
  That's the story of my life.
 Gmaj7   E
  That's the story of my life,
  Gmaj7 E
The story of my life. 𝄇 *Repeat ad lib. to fade*

Hand In Glove

Words & Music by
Morrissey & Johnny Marr

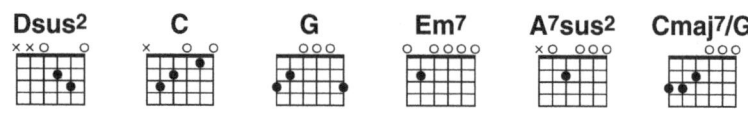

Capo third fret

Intro ‖: Dsus2 | C G | Dsus2 | C G :‖   *Play 3 times*

Verse 1
    Em7   A7sus2 C
   Hand in glove,
    Em7   A7sus2 Cmaj7/G
The sun shines out of our behinds.
    Em7   A7sus2
No it's not like any other love,
C   Em7   A7sus2 Cmaj7/G
This one is different because it's us!

Verse 2
    Em7   A7sus2 C
   Hand in glove,
    Em7   A7sus2 Cmaj7/G
We can go wherever we please.
    Em7   A7sus2 C
And everything depends upon
    Em7   A7sus2 Cmaj7/G
How near you stand to me.

Verse 3
    Em7   A7sus2 C
   And if the people stare,
    Em7   A7sus2
Then the people stare.
Cmaj7/G Em7
Oh,   I really don't know
              A7sus2 C Em7   A7sus2 Cmaj7/G
And I really don't care.

© Copyright 1983 Marr Songs Limited/Artane Music Incorporated.
Chrysalis Music Limited (50%)/Universal Music Publishing Limited (50%).
All Rights Reserved. International Copyright Secured.

Instrumental 1 ‖: **Dsus2** | **C G** | **Dsus2** | **C G** :‖

Verse 4
    Em7   **A7sus2** **C**
    Hand in glove,
      Em7   **A7sus2**
The good people laugh.
Cmaj7/G **Em7**   **A7sus2**
Yes, we   may be hidden by 'rags'
C   **Em7**   **A7sus2** **Cmaj7/G**
But we have something they'll never have.

Verse 5
    Em7   **A7sus2** **C**
    Hand in glove,
    Em7   **A7sus2**
The sun shines out of our behinds.
Cmaj7/G **Em7**   **A7sus2**
Yes, we   may be hidden by 'rags'
C   **Em7**   **A7sus2** **Cmaj7/G**
But we have something they'll never have.

Verse 6
Em7   **A7sus2** **C**
  And if the people stare,
    Em7   **A7sus2**
Then the people stare.
Cmaj7/G **Em7**
Oh,   I really don't know
          A7sus2 **C** **Em7**   **A7sus2** **Cmaj7/G**
And I really don't care.

Instrumental 2 ‖: **Dsus2** | **C G** | **Dsus2** | **C G** :‖

Verse 7
   Em7   **A7sus2** **C**
So hand in glove I stake my claim,
    Em7   **A7sus2**
I'll fight to the last breath.
Cmaj7/G **Em7**   **A7sus2**
If they   dare touch a hair on your head,
  C   **Em7**   **A7sus2**
I'll fight to the last breath.

Verse 8

      Cmaj7/G Em7   **A7sus2 C**
For   the   good life is out there somewhere
        Em7   **A7sus2 Cmaj7/G**
So stay on my arm, you little charmer.
        Em7   **A7sus2 C**
But I know my luck too well,
      Em7   **A7sus2 Cmaj7/G**
Yes, I know my luck too well.
        Em7   **A7sus2 C**
And I'll probably never see you again,
      Em7   **A7sus2 Cmaj7/G**
I'll probably never see you again,
      Em7   **A7sus2 C**   **Em7** **A7sus2 Cmaj7/G**
I'll probably never see   you again.

Instrumental 3 ‖: **Dsus2** | **C**   **G** | **Dsus2** | **C**   **G** :‖

Repeat to fade

Handsome Devil

Words & Music by
Morrissey & Johnny Marr

Am   F   G   Em   Fmaj7

Capo fourth fret

Intro | Am | Am | F | G |
       | Am | Am | F ||

Verse 1
     G   Am
All the streets are crammed with things,
   F
Eager to be held.
 G   Am
I know what hands are for,
            F
And I'd like to help myself.
G   Am
You ask me the time,
           F   G
But I sense something more.
             Am
And I would like to give you,
   F   G   Am
What I think you're asking for.
      F   G
You handsome devil,
Am   F   G
Oh, you handsome devil.

Chorus 1

```
         F     G     Am
Let me get my hands
   G       F    G         Am
On your      mammary glands,
         G           F                G
And let me get your head on the conjugal bed,
      Am     G    F      Em    Fmaj7  Em
         I say, I say, I say…
```

Verse 2

```
              Am
I crack the whip and you skip,
              F
But you deserve it,
        G                  Am        F    G
You deserve it, deserve it, deserve it.
       Am
A boy in the bush

Is worth two in the hand,
     F                             G
I think I can help you get through your exams,
Am                    F    G
   Oh, you handsome devil.
```

Chorus 2   As Chorus 1

Verse 3

```
              Am
I crack the whip and you skip,
              F
But you deserve it,
        G                  Am
You deserve it, deserve it, deserve it.
                                    F
And when we're in your scholarly room,
G            Am
Who will swallow whom?
                                    F
And when we're in your scholarly room
G            Am
Who will swallow whom?
                  F    G
You handsome devil.
```

Chorus 3   As Chorus 1

Verse 4
           Am
There's more to life than books you know,
    F   **G**
But not much more.
             Am
Oh, there's more to life than books you know,
    F
But not much more,
G
Not much more.
Am   **F**   **G**
  Oh, you handsome devil,
Am   **F**   **G**
  Oh, you handsome devil.

Coda | **F** | **G** | **Am**   ‖

The Hand That Rocks The Cradle

Words & Music by
Morrissey & Johnny Marr

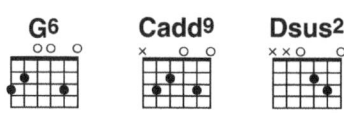

Capo second fret

Intro　　　　　‖: G6　　　| Cadd9　Dsus2 | G6　　　　　　| Cadd9　Dsus2 :‖
　　　　　　　　　　　　　　　　　　　　　　　　　　　　　　　　　Play 3 times

Verse 1
　　　　　(Dsus2)　　　G6　　　Cadd9
　　　　　Please don't cry,
　　　　　Dsus2　G6　　　　　　　　　Cadd9　Dsus2
　　　　　For the　ghost and the storm outside
　　　　　　　　　G6　　　　　　Cadd9　Dsus2
　　　　　Will not invade this sacred shrine,
　　　　　　　　　G6　　　　　　Cadd9　Dsus2
　　　　　Nor infiltrate your mind.
　　　　　　　　　G6　　　　　　Cadd9　Dsus2
　　　　　My life down I shall lie,
　　　　　　　　　G6　　　　　　　　Cadd9　Dsus2
　　　　　If the bogey-man should try
　　　　　　　　　G6　　　　　　Cadd9　　Dsus2
　　　　　To play tricks on your sacred mind
　　　　　　　　　G6　　　　　　Cadd9　Dsus2
　　　　　To tease, torment and tanta - lise.
　　　　　G6　　　　　　　Cadd9　Dsus2
　　　　　Wavering shadows loom,
　　　　　　　　　G6　　　　　　Cadd9　　Dsus2
　　　　　A piano plays in an empty room,
　　　　　　　　　　　G6　　　　　　　　Cadd9　Dsus2
　　　　　There'll be blood on the cleaver tonight.
　　　　　　　　　　　G6　　　　　　　　Cadd9　　Dsus2
　　　　　And when darkness lifts and the room is bright
　　　　　　　　　G6　　　　　　Cadd9　　Dsus2
　　　　　I'll still be by your side.
　　　　　　　　　G6　　　　　　Cadd9
　　　　　For you are all that matters,
　　　　　Dsus2　G6　　　　　　　　　Cadd9　　Dsus2
　　　　　And I'll love you till the day I die.

© Copyright 1984 De Sylva, Brown & Henderson Incorporated, USA/Marr Songs Limited/Artane Music Incorporated.
Chrysalis Music Limited (44.02%)/Universal Music Publishing Limited (44.03%)/
Redwood Music Limited (8.96%)/Campbell Connelly & Company Limited (2.99%).
All Rights Reserved. International Copyright Secured.

Chorus 1

      G⁶   Cadd⁹ Dsus²   G⁶   Cadd⁹ Dsus²
There never need be longing in your eyes,
    G⁶   Cadd⁹   Dsus² G⁶   Cadd⁹ Dsus²
As long as the hand that rocks the cradle is mine.

Verse 2

  G⁶   Cadd⁹ Dsus²
Ceiling shadows shimmy by,
        G⁶   Cadd⁹ Dsus²
And when the wardrobe towers like a beast of prey,
      G⁶   Cadd⁹ Dsus²
There's sadness in your beautiful eyes,
      G⁶   Cadd⁹   Dsus²
Oh your untouched, unsoiled, wondrous eyes.
     G⁶   Cadd⁹ Dsus²
My life down I shall lie,
      G⁶   Cadd⁹ Dsus²
Should restless spirits try,
    G⁶   Cadd⁹ Dsus²
To play tricks on your sacred mind,
  G⁶   Cadd⁹   Dsus²
I once had a child and it saved my life,
    G⁶   Cadd⁹ Dsus²
And I never even asked his name.
    G⁶   Cadd⁹   Dsus²
I just looked into his wondrous eyes
       G⁶   Cadd⁹ Dsus²
And said, "Never, never, never again."
    G⁶   Cadd⁹ Dsus²
And all too soon I did return,
G⁶   Cadd⁹ Dsus²
   Just like a moth to a flame,
    G⁶   Cadd⁹   Dsus²
So rattle my bones all over the stones,
      G⁶   Cadd⁹   Dsus²
I'm only a beggar-man whom nobody owns.
    G⁶   Cadd⁹ Dsus²
Oh, see how words as old as sin,
G⁶   Cadd⁹ Dsus²
Fit me like a glove.
    G⁶   Cadd⁹   Dsus²
I'm here and here I'll stay,
    G⁶   Cadd⁹   Dsus²
Together we lie, together we pray.

Chorus 2

      G6   Cadd9 Dsus2   G6   Cadd9 Dsus2
There never need be longing in your eyes,
    G6   Cadd9   Dsus2 G6   Cadd9 Dsus2
As long as the hand that rocks the cradle is mine,
    G6   Cadd9   Dsus2 G6   Cadd9 Dsus2
As long as the hand that rocks the cradle is mine, mine.

Verse 3

   G6   Cadd9 Dsus2   G6   Cadd9 Dsus2
Climb upon my knee,   sonny boy,
     G6   Cadd9 Dsus2   G6   Cadd9 Dsus2
Oh, though you're only three,   sonny boy, oh,
        G6   Cadd9
You're mine,
Dsus2   **G6**   Cadd9 Dsus2
And your mother she just never knew,
     G6   Cadd9
Oh, your mother, there's love,
Dsus2   **G6**   Cadd9 Dsus2
  There's love, there's love,
  G6   Cadd9 Dsus2
I did my best for her,
  G6   Cadd9 Dsus2
I did my best for her.
    G6   Cadd9 Dsus2
As long as there's love,
    G6   Cadd9 Dsus2
As long as there's love,
  G6   Cadd9 Dsus2
I did my best for her,
  G6   Cadd9 Dsus2
I did my best for her.

Instrumental   ‖: G6 | Cadd9 Dsus2 | G6 | Cadd9 Dsus2 :‖

To fade

The Headmaster Ritual

Words & Music by
Morrissey & Johnny Marr

A♭⁶⁄₉   C   C(add♯9)   B♭sus2   E♭maj7   F   G6

Am   Fmaj7   E7   Am/G   D/E   Cmaj7

Capo fourth fret

Intro | A♭⁶⁄₉ | C C(add♯9) C | A♭⁶⁄₉ | C C(add♯9) C |

| A♭⁶⁄₉ | B♭sus2 | E♭maj7 | A♭⁶⁄₉ |

||: C | C | C | C   :||

| E♭maj7 | A♭⁶⁄₉ | C | C |

| C | C | C | C |

| E♭maj7 | A♭⁶⁄₉ | C | C ||

Verse 1
    F   G6   C   Am
    Belligerent ghouls run Manchester schools,
Fmaj7   G6   C
Spineless swines, cemented minds.
          G6
Sir leads the troops, jealous of youth,
      Fmaj7   C   Am
Same old suit since nineteen sixty-two,
G6   E7
  He does the military two-step down the nape of my neck.

Chorus 1
  Am   Am/G
  I wanna go home,
E7   Fmaj7
  I don't wanna stay,
D/E   Cmaj7
  Give up education,
       Fmaj7 E7 F
Is a bad mistake.

© Copyright 1985 Marr Songs Limited/Artane Music Incorporated.
Chrysalis Music Limited (50%)/Universal Music Publishing Limited (50%).
All Rights Reserved. International Copyright Secured.

Verse 2

    Am   Am/G
   Mid-week on the   playing fields,
Em   Fmaj7
   Sir thwacks you on the knees,
              D/E   Cmaj7
Knees you in the groin, elbow in the face,
Fmaj7   E7
Bruises bigger than dinner plates.

Chorus 2

Fmaj7
  I wanna go home,
E7
I don't wanna stay.
A♭%   C   C(add♯9) C
Da-da-da-da-da-da-da - ee - ay - ay…

(w/vocal ad lib.) | A♭% | C C(add♯9) C | A♭% | B♭sus2 |
E♭maj7	A♭%	C C(add♯9) C	A♭%
C C(add♯9) C	A♭%	B♭sus2	E♭maj7
A♭%	C C(add♯9) C	A♭%	C C(add♯9) C
A♭%	B♭sus2	E♭maj7	A♭%	

Instrumental ||: C | C | C | C :||
| E♭maj7 | A♭% | C | C ||

Verse 3

  F   G6   C   Am
  Belligerent ghouls run Manchester schools
       Fmaj7   G6   C
Spineless bastards all …
      G6
Sir leads the troops, jealous of youth,
       Fmaj7   C   Am
Same old jokes since ninety-two,
G6   E7
  He does the military two-step down the nape of my neck.

Chorus 3

    Am   **Am/G**
  I wanna go home,
E7   **Fmaj7**
  I don't wanna stay,
D/E   **Cmaj7**
  Give up life
          Fmaj7 **E7** **F**
As a bad mistake.

Verse 4

    Am   **Am/G**
  "Please excuse me from gym,
Em   **Fmaj7**
  I've got this terrible cold coming on."
    D/E
He grabs and devours,
    Cmaj7
He kicks me in the showers.
Fmaj7
Kicks me in the showers
    E7
And he grabs and devours.

Chorus 4   As Chorus 2 *ad lib. to fade*

Heaven Knows I'm Miserable Now

Words & Music by
Morrissey & Johnny Marr

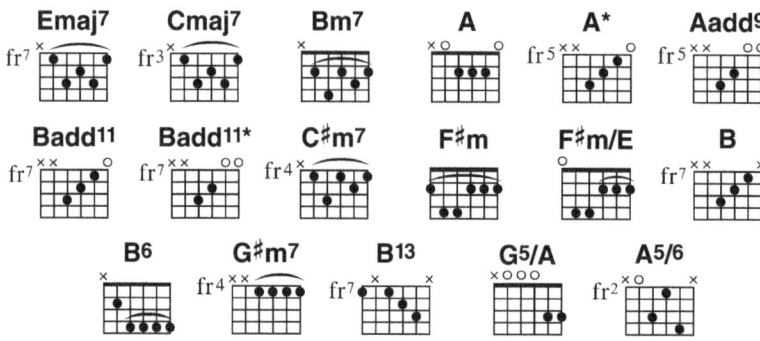

Capo second fret

Intro | Emaj7 | Cmaj7 | Bm7 | A |
| A* Aadd9 A* Aadd9 | Badd11 Badd11* Badd11 Badd11* |
| A* Aadd9 A* Aadd9 | Badd11 Badd11* Badd11 Badd11* ||

Verse 1
        Emaj7   C#m7
I was happy in the haze of a drunken hour,
    F#m   F#m/E   A*   B
But Heaven knows I'm miserable now.
     Emaj7   C#m7
I was looking for a job, and then I found a job,
   F#m   F#m/E   A*   Aadd9
And Heaven knows I'm miserable now.

Chorus 1
Emaj7 A* B
In my life,
Emaj7   A* G#m7
Why do I give valuable time
  C#m7   B6   A*   Emaj7 A* B A* G#m7
To people who don't care if I   live or die?

Instrumental 1 | C#m7 B6 | A* G#m7 | Aadd9 | B13 ||

© Copyright 1984 Marr Songs Limited/Artane Music Incorporated.
Chrysalis Music Limited (50%)/Universal Music Publishing Limited (50%).
All Rights Reserved. International Copyright Secured.

Verse 2

        Emaj7   C#m7
Two lovers entwined pass me by,
     F#m   F#m/E   A*   Aadd9
And Heaven knows I'm miserable now.
       Emaj7   C#m7
I was looking for a job, and then I found a job,
    F#m   F#m/E   A*   Aadd9
And Heaven knows I'm miserable now.

Chorus 2

Emaj7 C#m7
In my life,
F#m   F#m/E   B6
Why do I give valuable time
    Emaj7   C#m7   F#m F#m/E B6
To people who don't care if I   live or die?

Instrumental 2 | Emaj7 | Cmaj7 | Bm7 | A |

| A* Aadd9 A* Aadd9 | Badd11 Badd11* Badd11 Badd11* |

| A* Aadd9 A* Aadd9 | Badd11 Badd11* Badd11 Badd11* ||

Verse 3

        Emaj7   C#m7
What she asked of me at the end of the day:
   F#m F#m/E   A*   B
Caligula would have blushed.
      Emaj7   C#m7
"You've been in the house too long," she said,
   F#m F#m/E   A*   Aadd9
And I   naturally fled.

Chorus 3

Emaj7 A* B
In my life,
Emaj7   A*   G#m7
Why do I smile
   C#m7   B6   A*   Emaj7   A* B A* G#m7
At people who I'd much rather   kick in the eye?

Instrumental 3 | C#m7 B6 | A* G#m7 | Aadd9 | B13 | ||

Verse 4

    Emaj7   C♯m7
I was happy in the haze of a drunken hour,
  F♯m   F♯m/E   A* Aadd9
But Heaven knows I'm miserable now.
    Emaj7   C♯m7
"You've been in the house too long," she said,
  F♯m F♯m/E   B6
And I (naturally) fled.

Chorus 4

Emaj7 C♯m7
In my life,
F♯m   F♯m/E   B6
Why do I give valuable time
   Emaj7   C♯m7   F♯m F♯m/E B6
To people who don't care if I live or die?

Coda

‖: Emaj7 | C♯m7 | F♯m F♯m/E | B6 :‖

| Emaj7 | Cmaj7 | Emaj7 | G5/A |

| A5/6 ‖

How Soon Is Now?

Words & Music by
Morrissey & Johnny Marr

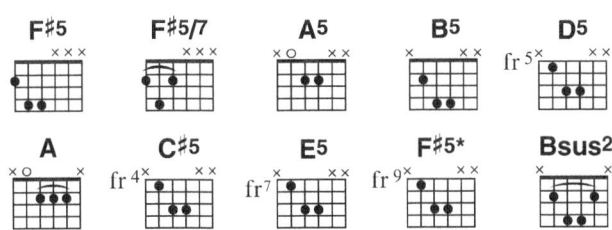

Intro
| F#5   F#5/7 | F#5   F#5/7 | F#5   F#5/7 | A5   B5 |
| F#5   F#5/7 | F#5   F#5/7 | F#5   F#5/7 | A5   B5 ||

Verse 1
    F#riff
I am the son and the heir
  A5   **B5**   **F#riff**
Of a shyness that is criminally vulgar,

I am the son and heir
                A5   **B5**
Of nothing in particular.

Chorus 1
B5 **D5**   **A**
    You shut your mouth,
Esus4
How can you say
C#5   **E5**   **F#5***
   I go about things the wrong way?
Bsus2   **A**   **Esus4**
I am human and I need to be loved,
C#5   **E5**   **F#riff**
Just like everybody else does.

Instrumental 1
| F#5   F#5/7 | F#5   F#5/7 | F#5   F#5/7 | A5   B5 |
| F#5   F#5/7 | F#5   F#5/7 | F#5   F#5/7 | A5   B5 ||

© Copyright 1984 Universal Music Publishing Limited (50%)/Copyright Control (50%).
All Rights Reserved. International Copyright Secured.

Verse 2   As Verse 1

Chorus 2   As Chorus 1

Instrumental 2 ‖: F♯5   F♯5/7 | F♯5   F♯5/7 | F♯5   F♯5/7 | A5   B5 |

| F♯5   F♯5/7 | F♯5   F♯5/7 | F♯5   F♯5/7 | A5   B5   :‖

                B5   D5   A
Bridge   There's a club, if you'd like to go,
        Esus4   C♯5   E5   F♯5
You could meet somebody who really loves you,
           Bsus2
So you go, and you stand on your own,
 A   Esus4
   And you leave on your own,
     C♯5   E5   F♯riff
And you go home, and you cry and you want to die.

Instrumental 3 ‖: F♯5   F♯5/7 | F♯5   F♯5/7 | F♯5   F♯5/7 | A5   B5 |

| F♯5   F♯5/7 | F♯5   F♯5/7 | F♯5   F♯5/7 | A5   B5   :‖

          B5   D5   A Esus4
Chorus 3   When you say it's gonna happen now,
C♯5   E5   F♯5*
   Well, when exactly do you mean?
        Bsus2   A   Esus4
See, I've already waited too long,
C♯5   E5   F♯riff
And all my hope is gone.

Instrumental 4 ‖: F♯5 | F♯5/7 | F♯5 | F♯5/7 | F♯5 | F♯5/7 | A5 | B5 |

| F♯5 | F♯5/7 | F♯5 | F♯5/7 | F♯5 | F♯5/7 | A5 | B5 :‖

| B5 | D5 | A | Esus4 | C♯5 | E5 | F♯5* |

| B5 | D5 | A | Esus4 | C♯5 | E5 | F♯5 | F♯5/7 |

‖: F♯5 | F♯5/7 | F♯5 | F♯5/7 | F♯5 | F♯5/7 | A5 | B5 |

| F♯5 | F♯5/7 | F♯5 | F♯5/7 | F♯5 | F♯5/7 | A5 | B5 :‖

Chorus 4   As Chorus 1

Coda   ‖: F♯5 | F♯5/7 | F♯5 | F♯5/7 | F♯5 | F♯5/7 | A5 | B5 |

| F♯5 | F♯5/7 | F♯5 | F♯5/7 | F♯5 | F♯5/7 | A5 | B5 :‖

To fade

I Don't Owe You Anything

Words & Music by
Morrissey & Johnny Marr

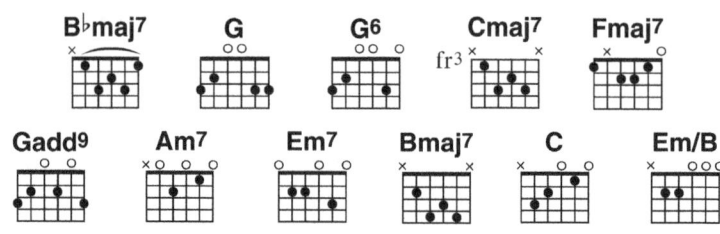

Capo fourth fret

Intro | B♭maj7 | G   G6 | Cmaj7 | Cmaj7 ||

Verse 1
(Cmaj7)
Bought on stolen wine,

A nod was the first step.
                   Fmaj7
You knew very well
   Gadd9   Cmaj7
What was coming next.

Verse 2   As Verse 1

Chorus 1
      Fmaj7   Gadd9   Cmaj7   Bmaj7
Did I really walk all this way,
B♭maj7 Gadd9   Cmaj7
Just to hear you say:
         Fmaj7   Gadd9   Cmaj7   Bmaj7
"Oh, I don't want to go out   tonight,"
      B♭maj7   Gadd9   Am7
"Oh, I don't want to go out   tonight."

Oh, but you will,
    B♭maj7   Gadd9   Cmaj7
For you must.
Em7   C   Em/B   Fmaj7   Am7   G6   Am7
I don't owe you anything,   no,
Em7   C   Em/B   Fmaj7
But you owe me something,
      B♭maj7
Repay me now.

© Copyright 1984 Marr Songs Limited/Artane Music Incorporated.
Chrysalis Music Limited (50%)/Universal Music Publishing Limited (50%).
All Rights Reserved. International Copyright Secured.

Verse 3

  Gadd9   **Cmaj7**
   You should never go to them,

  Let them come to you,
    Fmaj7
  Just like I do,
  Gadd9 **Cmaj7**
   Just like I do.

Verse 4

      (Cmaj7)
  You should not go to them,

  Let them come to you,
    Fmaj7
  Just like I do,
  Gadd9 **Cmaj7**
   Just like I do.

Chorus 2 As Chorus 1

Verse 5

  Gadd9 **Cmaj7**
   Too freely on your lips,

  Words prematurely sad,
    Fmaj7   **Gadd9**   **Cmaj7**
  Oh, but I know what will make you smile tonight.

Verse 6

    (Cmaj7)
  Life is never kind,

  Life is never kind,
    Fmaj7   **Gadd9**   **(Cmaj7)**
  Oh, but I know what will make you smile tonight.

Coda

| Cmaj7 | Cmaj7 | Cmaj7 | Cmaj7 Bmaj7 |
| B♭maj7 | Gadd9 | Cmaj7 (𝄐) | ‖ |

I Keep Mine Hidden

Words & Music by
Morrissey & Johnny Marr

C   F   Dm   Am   B♭   Em

Intro

| C | C | F   Dm | Am B♭ C |

| F   Dm | Am B♭ C | F   Dm | Am B♭ C |

| F   Dm ||

Verse 1

Am B♭   C   F   Dm
    Hate, love and war,
Am B♭   C   F   Dm
Force e - motions to the fore.
Am B♭   C F   Dm
But not for me, of course,
   Am B♭ C   F
Of course I   keep mine hidden.
B♭   F
Oh…

Chorus 1

  C   F
  I keep mine hidden
  C   F
But it's so easy for you,
          Em
Because you let yours flail
      Am
Into public view.
B♭ C |C |
Oh, oh ...

© Copyright 1995 Marr Songs Limited/Artane Music Incorporated.
Chrysalis Music Limited (50%)/Universal Music Publishing Limited (50%).
All Rights Reserved. International Copyright Secured.

Verse 2

```
        F         Dm    Am   B♭  C
Yellow and green, a stumbling block,
        F           Dm     Am    B♭  C
I'm a twenty-digit combination to   unlock.
        F          Dm    Am
With a past where to be 'touched'
B♭   C   F        Dm    Am   B♭  C
Meant to be 'mental'.
```

Instrumental | F   Dm | Am B♭ C | F   Dm | Am B♭ C |

| F   Dm | Am B♭ C | F   B♭ | F ||

Chorus 2

```
C                 F
Ooh, I keep mine hidden,
      C                 F
The lies are so easy for you.
              Em
Because you let yours slide
         Am
Into public view.
B♭   C
Oh,  oh…
```

| C | C | C | C ||

```
         F
Use your loaf!
```

I Know It's Over

Words & Music by
Morrissey & Johnny Marr

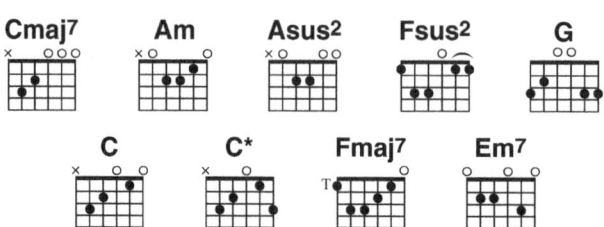

Verse 1

        Cmaj7   **Am**
Oh mother, I can feel the soil falling over my head.
Asus2 Fsus2 G   Cmaj7
                And as I climb into an empty bed,
C   **Asus2**
Oh well,   enough said.
Fsus2 G   **Fsus2**   **G**
     I know it's over, still I cling,
Fsus2   **G**
I don't know where else I can go, mother…

| **Fsus2**   **G**   **Fsus2 G** |

Verse 2

        Cmaj7   **Asus2**
Oh mother, I can feel the soil falling over my head,
Fsus2 G   **Cmaj7**
         See, the sea wants to take me,
                          C   **Cmaj7**
The knife wants to slit me
       Asus2
Do you think you can help me?
Fsus2 G   **C**
Sad   veiled bride, please be happy
                                  Asus2
Handsome groom, give her room.
Fsus2 G   **Cmaj7**
Loud, loutish lover, treat her kindly
                  C*   **Asus2**   **Am**
Though she needs you more_____ than she loves you.

© Copyright 1986 Marr Songs Limited/Artane Music Incorporated.
Chrysalis Music Limited (50%)/Universal Music Publishing Limited (50%).
All Rights Reserved. International Copyright Secured.

Chorus 1

            Fsus2
And I know it's over,
  G
Still I cling,
 Fsus2   **G**
I don't know where else I can go.
    Fsus2   **G**
It's over, it's over, it's over…
Fsus2 **G**   **C**
   I know it's over,
             Fsus2
And it never really began.
G   **Fsus2** **G** **Am**
  But in my heart it was so real,
Fsus2   **G**   **Fsus2** **G**
  And you even spoke to me and said:

Verse 3

 Cmaj7   **C**
  "If you're so funny,
 Cmaj7   **Asus2**   **Fmaj7** **G**
  Then why are you on your own tonight?
   C
And if you're so clever,
   Cmaj7   **Asus2**
Then why are you on your own tonight?
Fmaj7 **G**   **C**
If   you're so very entertaining,
   Cmaj7   **Asus2**
Then why are you on your own tonight?
Fmaj7 **G**   **C**
If   you're so very good looking,
Cmaj7   **Asus2**   **Am**
Why do you sleep alone tonight?
     Fmaj7 **G** **C**   **Cmaj7**
I know, 'cos   tonight is just like any other night
C   **Cmaj7**   **Asus2**   **Am**
  That's why you're on your own tonight,
Fmaj7 **G**   **C**   **Cmaj7**
    With your triumphs and your charms
  C **Cmaj7**   **Asus2**   **Am**
  While   they're in each other's arms…"

Chorus 2

    Fsus2   **G**   **Fsus2**
    It's so easy to laugh,
                G
It's so easy to hate,
      Fsus2   **G**
It takes strength to be gentle and kind
      Fsus2   **G**
It's over, over, over…
Fsus2 **G**   **C**
  It's so easy to laugh
       Fsus2
It's so easy to hate
    G   **Fsus2** **G**
It takes guts to be gentle and kind
Am   **G**
Over, over…
Fsus2 **G**   **C**   **Fsus2** **G**
  Love is natural and real,
   Fsus2 **G** **Em7**
But not   for you, my love,
  Fsus2
Not tonight my love.
G   **C**   **Fsus2** **G**
  Love is natural and real,
   Fsus2 **G**   **Em7** **Fsus2** **G**
But not for such as you and I,   my love.

Coda

  Fsus2 **G** **C**   **Fsus2** **G**   **Fsus2** **G** **Em7**
‖:   Oh mother, I can feel the soil falling over my head,
Fsus2 **G**   **C**   **Fsus2** **G**   **Fsus2** **G** **Em7**
Oh_____ mother, I can feel the soil falling over my head,
Fsus2 **G**   **C**   **Fsus2** **G**   **Fsus2** **G** **Em7**
Oh_____ mother, I can feel the soil falling over my head… :‖

Repeat ad lib. to fade

I Want The One I Can't Have

Words & Music by
Morrissey & Johnny Marr

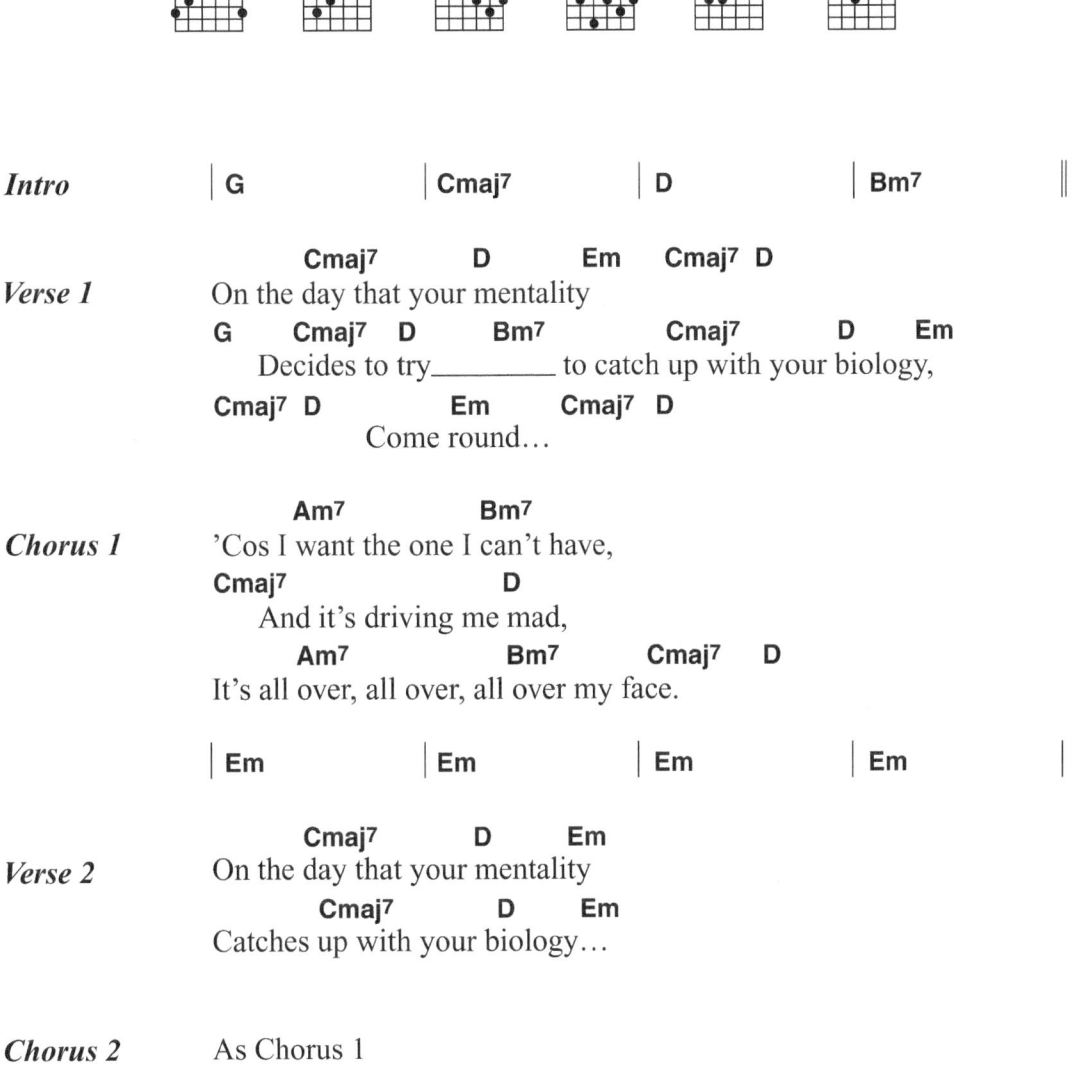

Bridge 1

   G   Cmaj7 D   Bm7
   A double bed and a stalwart lover for sure,
Cmaj7   D   Em Cmaj7 D
These are the riches of the poor.
   G   Cmaj7 D   Bm7
   A double bed and a stalwart lover for sure,
Cmaj7   D   Em Cmaj7 D | Em |Cmaj7 D
These are the riches of the poor.

Chorus 3 As Chorus 1

Verse 3

     Cmaj7   D   Em Cmaj7 D
A tough kid who sometimes swallows nails,
Cmaj7 D   Em Cmaj7 D
Raised on Prisoner's Aid,
     Am7   Bm7
He killed a policeman when he was thirteen
    Cmaj7   D
And somehow that really impressed me,
   Am7 Bm7 Cmaj7 D
And it's written all over my face.

Bridge 2 | G | Cmaj7 | D | Bm7 ||

    Cmaj7   D   Em Cmaj7 D
Oh, these are the riches of the poor,

     | G | Cmaj7 | D | Bm7 |

Cmaj7   D   Em Cmaj7 D | Em |Cmaj7 D
These are the riches of the poor.

Chorus 4 As Chorus 1

Verse 4

      Cmaj7   **D**   **Em**
On the day that your mentality
      Cmaj7   **D**   **Em**   **Cmaj7** **D**
Catches up with your biology…
      Am7   **Bm7**
And if you ever need self-validation,
    Cmaj7   **D**
Just meet me in the alley by the railway station,
  Am7   **Bm7**   **Cmaj7**   **D**
   It's all over my face._____

Coda

| Em | Em | Em | Em |
| Em | Em | Em | Em |
| Em | ‖

I Started Something I Couldn't Finish

Words & Music by
Morrissey & Johnny Marr

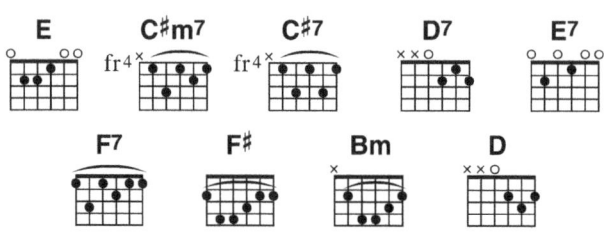

Intro
E	N.C.	E	E N.C.
C♯m7	C♯m7	C♯7	C♯7
D7	E7 F7	F♯	F♯	

Verse 1

    Bm
The lanes were silent,
    D   **E**   **F♯**
There was nothing, no-one, nothing around for miles.
    Bm
I doused a friendly venture,
    D   **E**
With a hard-faced three-word gesture.

Chorus 1

  C♯m7
    I started something,
C♯7
Forced you into a zone,
     D7   **E7**   **F7**   **F♯**
And you were clearly never meant to go.
C♯m7
    Hair brushed and parted,
    C♯7
Typical me, typical me, typical me,
   D7   **E7**   **F♯**
I started something and now I'm not too sure.

© Copyright 1987 Marr Songs Limited/Artane Music Incorporated.
Chrysalis Music Limited (50%)/Universal Music Publishing Limited (50%).
All Rights Reserved. International Copyright Secured.

Verse 2

    Bm
I grabbed you by the guilded beams,
 D   **E**   **F♯**
   That's what Tradition means.
    Bm
And I doused another venture,
     D   **E**
With a gesture that was absolutely vile.

Chorus 2   As Chorus 1

Verse 3

    Bm
I grabbed you by the guilded beams,
 D   **E**   **F♯**
   That's what Tradition means.
        Bm
And now eighteen months' hard-labour
    D E
Seems   fair enough.

Chorus 3   As Chorus 1

C♯m7
   I started something,
C♯7 | **D7** | **E7** **F7** | **F♯** |
   I started something,
     C♯m7
Typical me, typical me, typical me, typical me,
   C♯7
Typical me, typical me, typical me,
    D7   **E7**   **F7**   **F♯**
I started something   and now I'm not too sure.

Coda | **C♯m7** | **C♯m7** | **C♯7** | **C♯7** |

        | **D7** | **E7** **F7** | **F♯** | **F♯** ||

                                                                  To fade

I Won't Share You

Words & Music by
Morrissey & Johnny Marr

G Am C D7 Bm Em

**Capo twelfth fret
(optional)**

Chorus 1

    G Am   C   D7
    I won't share you,
    G Am   C   D7
    I won't share you
          G   Am   C D7
With the drive, the ambition and the zeal I feel,
        G   Am C   D7
This is my time.

Verse 1

    Bm
The note I wrote:
      Em
As she read, she said,
    C   D7
"Has the Perrier gone straight to my head,
  Bm   Em
Or is life sick and cruel instead?"

"Yes!"
C
No, no, no, no, no, no,
D7   C D7
No, no, no, no, no, no…

Chorus 2

    G Am   C   D7
    I won't share you,
    G Am   C   D7
    I won't share you
          G   Am   C D7
With the drive and the dreams inside,
        G   Am C   D7
This is my time.

© Copyright 1987 Marr Songs Limited/Artane Music Incorporated.
Chrysalis Music Limited (50%)/Universal Music Publishing Limited (50%).
All Rights Reserved. International Copyright Secured.

Verse 2

      Bm   **Em**
Life tends to come and go,
C   **D7**
That's OK as long as you know.
     Bm   **Em**
Life tends to come and go,
              C
As long as you know, no, no, no, no, no,
D7   **C** **D7**
No, no, no, no…

Chorus 3   As Chorus 2

Verse 3

           Bm   **Em**
I want the freedom and I want the guile,
        C   **D7**
I want the freedom and the guile,
        Bm   **Em**
Oh, life tends to come and go,
              C
As long as you know, no, no, no, no, no,
D7   **C** **D7**
No, no, no, no…

Chorus 4

   G **Am**   **C**   **D7**
I_____ won't share you,
   G **Am**   **C**
I_____ won't share you
 D7   **G**
I'll see you somewhere,
 Am   **C**   **D7**
  I'll see you some time, but…

Coda

G	Am	C	D7
Em	Bm	C	D7	

To fade

Is It Really So Strange?

Words & Music by
Morrissey & Johnny Marr

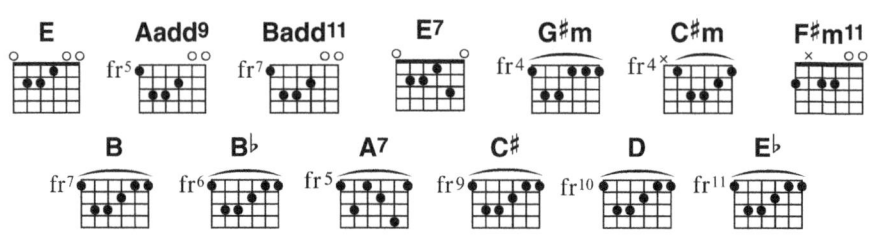

| Intro | \| E | \| E | \| E | \| **Aadd9 Badd11** \|\| |

Verse 1
              E
I left the North,

I travelled South,

I found a tiny house,
      Aadd9   **Badd11**
And I can't help the way I feel.

\| E7   \| E7   \| E7   \|

Aadd9 Badd11 E
Oh, yes you can kick me,

And you can punch me.

And you can break my face,
      Aadd9   **Badd11**   **E**
But you won't change the way that I feel,
  Aadd9   **E**
   'Cos I love you.

© Copyright 1986 Marr Songs Limited/Artane Music Incorporated.
Chrysalis Music Limited (50%)/Universal Music Publishing Limited (50%).
All Rights Reserved. International Copyright Secured.

Chorus 1

              G♯m   C♯m F♯m11 Badd11   E
And is it really   so   strange?
              G♯m   C♯m F♯m11 Badd11   E
Oh is it really   so   strange?
              G♯m   C♯m   F♯m11 B B♭
Oh is it really so, really so strange?
A7   B♭ B
  I say no, you say yes,
              C♯ D   E♭
(And you will change your mind!)

Verse 2

       E♭   E
I left the South,

I travelled North,

I got confused - I killed a horse,
  Aadd9   Badd11
I can't help the way I feel.

| E7 | E7 | E7 | |

Aadd9 Badd11 E
Oh, yes you can punch me,

And you can butt me,

And you can break my spine,
         Aadd9   Badd11   E
But you won't change the way I feel
Aadd9   E
  'Cos I love you.

Chorus 2   As Chorus 1

Instrumental | E | E7 | E | Aadd9 Badd11 ‖

79

Verse 3

              E
I left the North again,

I travelled South again,

And I got confused: I killed a man,
    Aadd9   **Badd11**
And I can't help the way I feel,

| **E7** | **E7** | **E7** | |

  Aadd9   **Badd11** **E**
I can't help the way I   feel,

| **E7** | **E7** | **E7** | |

  Aadd9   **Badd11** **E**
I can't help the way I feel,
Aadd9   **E7**
   I lost my bag in Newport Pagnell.

Chorus 3

            G#m   **C#m**   **F#m11**   **Badd11**   **E**
Why is the last   mile the hardest mile?
    G#m   **C#m**   **F#m11**   **Badd11**   **E**
My throat was dry, with the sun in my eyes.
      G#m   **C#m**   **F#m11** **B** **Bb**
And I realised,   I realised,
A7   **Bb**   **B**   **C#**
   That I could never, I could never, never, never
D   **Eb**   **E**
Go back home again.

Jeane

Words & Music by
Morrissey & Johnny Marr

C   G   Fmaj9   Am   Em7

Capo second fret

Intro

‖: C   G | C   G | C   G | C   G :‖

| Fmaj9 | G   Am   G | C   G | C   G ‖

Verse 1

```
     C   G  C  G
Jeane,
        C          G     C    G
The low-life has lost its appeal.
          Fmaj9        G   Am
And I'm tired of walking these streets,
G   C                G  C   G
To a room with its cupboard bare.
C    G  C   G
Jeane,
     C          G         C   G
I'm not sure what happiness means.
        Fmaj9          G   Am  G
But I look in your eyes and I know
C         G  C   G
   That it isn't there.
```

Chorus 1

```
        Fmaj9  G   C    G
We tried,     we failed,
        Fmaj9  G      C   G
We tried,     and we failed,
        Fmaj9        G
We tried and we failed,
        C            G
We tried and we failed,
        Fmaj9      G
We tried…
```

© Copyright 1983 Marr Songs Limited/Artane Music Incorporated.
Chrysalis Music Limited (50%)/Universal Music Publishing Limited (50%).
All Rights Reserved. International Copyright Secured.

Verse 2

       C   G   C   G
Jeane,
                C   G   C   G
There's ice on the sink where we bathe.
       Fmaj9   G   Am G
So how can you call this a home,
C   G   C   G
  When you know it's a grave?
         C   G   C   G
But you still hold a greedy grace,
C   G   C   G
  As you tidy the place.
Fmaj9   G   Am
But it will never be clean,
G C   G C   G
Jeane.

Chorus 2   As Chorus 1

Verse 3

           C   G C   G
Cash on the nail,
C   G   C
  It's just a fairytale.
G   **Fmaj9**   G   Am G
And I don't believe in magic any more,

|C   G |C   G |

C   G   C   G
  But I think you know,
C   G   C   G
  I really think you know,
Fmaj9   G   Am G
  I think you know the truth,
C   G C   G
Jeane.

Instrumental | Em7 | Em7 | Em7 | Em7 |

|C   G |C   G |C   G |C   G‖

Verse 4

     Fmaj⁹   **G**   **Am G**
  No heavenly choir,
        C   **G**   **C**   **G**
Not for me and not for you.
C   **G**   **C**   **G**
  Because I think that you know,
C   **G**   **C**   **G**
  I really think you know,
Fmaj⁹   **G**   **Am**
  I think you know the truth
G **C**   **G** **C**   **G**
Jeane.

Chorus 3

       Fmaj⁹ **G**   **C** **G**
That we tried,   and we failed,
       Fmaj⁹ **G**   **C** **G**
That we tried,   and we failed,
    Fmaj⁹   **G**
We tried and we failed,
    C   **G**
We tried and we failed
  Fmaj⁹ G C
Oh   Jeane.

Last Night I Dreamt That Somebody Loved Me

Words & Music by
Morrissey & Johnny Marr

Capo seventh fret

Verse 1
    Am   **F**
    Last night I dreamt
Fm13   **Em7**   **E7**
    That somebody loved me.
Am   **F**
    No hope, no harm,
              Fm13   **Em7**   **E7**
    Just another false alarm.
Am   **F**
    Last night I felt
Fm13   **Em7**   **E7**
    Real arms around me.
Am   **F**
    No hope, no harm,
              Fm13   **Em7**
    Just another false alarm.

© Copyright 1987 Marr Songs Limited/Artane Music Incorporated.
Chrysalis Music Limited (50%)/Universal Music Publishing Limited (50%).
All Rights Reserved. International Copyright Secured.

Verse 2

   E7   Am
So, tell me how long
   F   Fm13 Em7
Before the last one?
   E7   Am
And tell me how long
   F   Fm13 Em7
Before the right one?
   E7 Am F
This story is old, I know,
     Fm13 Em7
But it goes on.
   E7 Am F
This story is old, I know,
     Fm13 Em7 E7
But it goes on.

Coda   ‖: Am | F | Fm13 | Em7 E7 :‖
                               Repeat ad lib. & to fade

London

Words & Music by
Morrissey & Johnny Marr

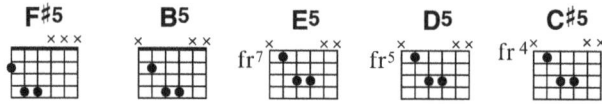

Intro | F#5 | F#5 | F#5 | F#5 ||

Verse 1
   (F#5)
Smoke lingers 'round your fingers,

Train heave on to Euston.
     B5
Do you think you've made
  E5   (F#5)
The right decision this time?

Instrumental | F#5 | F#5 | B5 | E5 |
                              Oh ...
| F#5 | F#5 | F#5 | F#5 ||

Verse 2
   (F#5)
You left your tired family grieving,

And you think they're sad because you're leaving.
      B5
But did you see Jealousy in the eyes
  E5   F#5
Of the ones who had to stay behind?
     B5
And do you think you've made
  E5   (F#5)
The right decision this time?

| F#5 | F#5 | F#5 | F#5 ||

© Copyright 1986 Marr Songs Limited/Artane Music Incorporated.
Chrysalis Music Limited (50%)/Universal Music Publishing Limited (50%).
All Rights Reserved. International Copyright Secured.

Verse 3

    (F♯5)
You left your girlfriend on the platform,

With this really ragged notion that you'll return.
  B5
But she knows,
    E5   F♯5
That when he goes he really goes.
  B5
And do you think you've made
 E5   F♯5
The right decision this time?

Coda ‖: F♯5 D5 E5 | C♯5 D5 E5 | F♯5 D5 E5 | C♯5 D5 E5 :‖

Repeat to fade

Meat Is Murder

Words & Music by
Morrissey & Johnny Marr

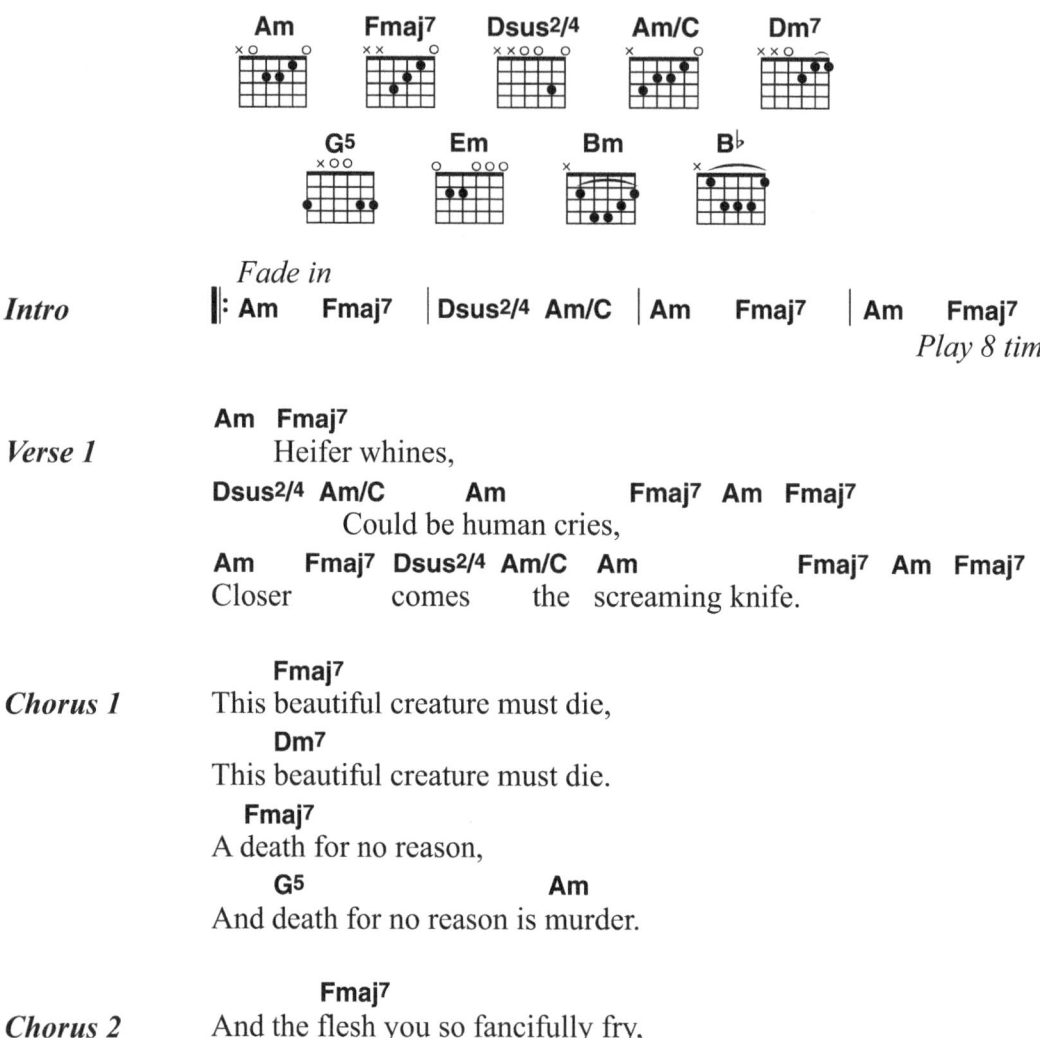

Intro
```
Fade in
||: Am   Fmaj7  | Dsus2/4  Am/C | Am   Fmaj7  | Am   Fmaj7  :||
                                                    Play 8 times
```

Verse 1

    Am Fmaj7
      Heifer whines,
Dsus2/4 Am/C   **Am**   **Fmaj7 Am Fmaj7**
      Could be human cries,
Am   **Fmaj7 Dsus2/4 Am/C Am**   **Fmaj7 Am Fmaj7**
Closer   comes   the screaming knife.

Chorus 1

    Fmaj7
This beautiful creature must die,
    Dm7
This beautiful creature must die.
    Fmaj7
A death for no reason,
    G5   **Am**
And death for no reason is murder.

Chorus 2

    Fmaj7
And the flesh you so fancifully fry,
    Dm7
Is not succulent, tasty or kind.
    Fmaj7
It's death for no reason,
    Dm7   **Am**
And death for no reason is murder.
    Fmaj7   **Em**   **Dm7 Fmaj7**   **Am**
And the calf that you carve with a smile is   murder,
    Fmaj7   **Em**   **Dm7 Fmaj7**   **Am**
And the turkey you festively slice is   murder.

© Copyright 1985 Marr Songs Limited/Artane Music Incorporated.
Chrysalis Music Limited (50%)/Universal Music Publishing Limited (50%).
All Rights Reserved. International Copyright Secured.

Bridge

   C   Bm B♭
   Do you know how animals die?

| Am Fmaj7 | Dsus2/4 Am/C |

Am   Fmaj7
Kitchen aromas aren't very homely,
   Dm7
It's not comforting, cheery or kind.
 Fmaj7   G5   Am
It's sizzling blood and the unholy stench of murder.

Chorus 3

   Fmaj7
It's not natural, normal or kind.
 Dm7
The flesh you so fancifully fry,
  Fmaj7   Em
The meat in your mouth,
   Dm7 Fmaj7 Am
As you savour the flavour of murder.
Fmaj7 Em Dm7 Fmaj7 Am
No, no, no, it's   murder,
Fmaj7 Em Dm7 Fmaj7 Am   C
No, no, no, it's   murder.

Coda

    Bm   B♭
And who hears when animals cry?

‖: Am Fmaj7 | Dsus2/4 Am/C | Am Fmaj7 | Am Fmaj7 :‖
                 Repeat ad lib. to fade

Money Changes Everything

Words & Music by
Johnny Marr

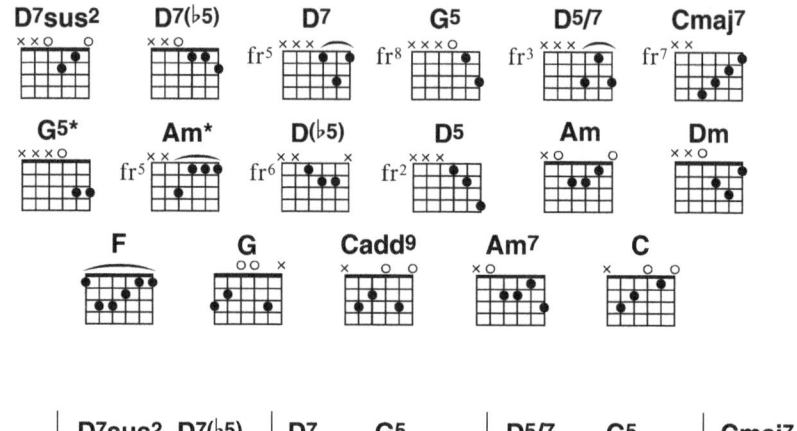

Intro	| D7sus2 D7(♭5) | D7 G5	| D5/7 G5	| Cmaj7 G5*	|
	| Am* D(♭5) | D5/7 G5	| D5/7 G5	| D5	||
Verse 1	| Am	| Am	| Am	| Am |
	| Am	| Am	| Am	| Am |
	| Am	| Am	| Am	| Am ||
Chorus 1	| Dm	| F G	| Am	| Am |
	| Dm	| F G	| Am	| Am ||
Verse 2	| Am	| Am	| Am	| Am |
	| Am	| Am	| Am	| Am ||
Chorus 2	As Chorus 1			
Bridge 1	| D7sus2 D7(♭5) | D7 G5	| D5/7 G5	| Cmaj7 G5*	|
	| Am* D(♭5) | D5/7 G5	| D5/7 G5	| D5	||
Verse 3	As Verse 2			
Chorus 3	As Chorus 1			

© Copyright 1986 Marr Songs Limited.
Universal Music Publishing Limited.
All Rights Reserved. International Copyright Secured.

Bridge 2	| F	G	| Am	Cadd⁹	| F	G	| Am⁷	C	|
	| F	G	| Am	Cadd⁹	| F	G	| Am⁷		||
Chorus 4	| Dm		| F	G	| Dm		| F	G	|
	| Dm		| F	G	| Am		| Am		||
Verse 4	| Am		| Am		| Am		| Am		|
	| Am		| Am		||				
Chorus 5	| Dm		| F	G	| Dm		| F	G	|
	| Dm		| F	G	| Am		| Am		||
Coda	| Am		| Am		| Am		| Am		|
	| Am		| Am		| Am		| Am		|
	| Am		| Am		| Am		| Am		||

To fade

Miserable Lie

Words & Music by
Morrissey & Johnny Marr

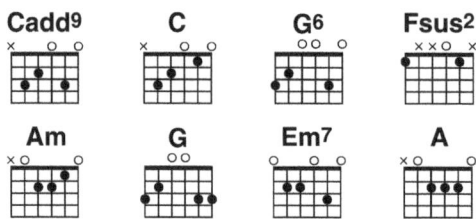

Capo second fret

Intro | Cadd9   C | G6   Fsus2 | Cadd9   C | G6   Fsus2 ‖

Verse 1
          Cadd9   C   G6   Fsus2
So, goodbye,
    Cadd9   C   G6   Fsus2   Cadd9   C   G6   Fsus2
    Please stay with   your own kind,
      Cadd9 C G6 Fsus2   Cadd9 C
And I'll   stay with mine.
G6   Fsus2   Cadd9 C
There's something against us,
G6   Fsus2   Cadd9 C
    It's not time,
G6   Fsus2   Cadd9 C   G6   Fsus2
    It's not time.
        Cadd9   C   G6   Fsus2   Cadd9   C   G6   Fsus2
So, goodbye, goodbye, goodbye, goodbye…

Verse 2
      Am   G   Em7
I know I need hardly say,
         Am   G   Em7
How much I love your casual way.
      Am   G   Em7
Oh, but please put your tongue away,
      Am   G   Em7
A little higher and we're well away.
      Am   G   Em7
The dark nights are drawing in,
      Am   G   Em7
And your humour is as black as them.

© Copyright 1984 Marr Songs Limited/Artane Music Incorporated.
Chrysalis Music Limited (50%)/Universal Music Publishing Limited (50%).
All Rights Reserved. International Copyright Secured.

Verse 2
(cont.)

       Am   **G** **Em7**
    I look at yours, you laugh at mine,
      Am   **G** **Em7**
    And 'love' is just a miserable lie.
        Am   **G** **Em7**
    You have destroyed my flower-like life,
       Am   **G** **Em7**
    Not once: twice.
       Am   **G** **Em7**
    You have corrupt my innocent mind,
       Am   **G** **Em7**
    Not once: twice.
       Am   **G** **Em7**
    I know the wind-swept mystical air,
      Am   **G** **Em7**
    It means I'd like to see your underwear.
      Am   **G** **Em7**
    I recognise that mystical air,
      Am   **G** **Em7**
    It means I'd like to seize your underwear.
      Am   **G** **Em7**
    What do we get for our trouble and pain?
      Am   **G** **Em7**
    Just a rented room in Whalley Range.
      Am   **G**
    What do we get for our trouble and pain?
    Em7 **Am**   **G** **Em7**
    …Whalley Range!
      Am   **G** **Em7**
    Into the depths of the criminal world
       Am **G** **Em7**
    I followed her…

Instrumental 1 | **Am** | **G**   **Em7** | **Am** | **G**   **Em7** ‖

Verse 3

      Am   **G** **Em7** **Am** **G** **Em7**
    I need advice, I need advice.
      Am   **G** **Em7**
    I need advice, I need advice.
      Am   **G** **Em7**
    Nobody ever looks at me twice,
      Am **G** **Em7** **Am** **G** **Em7**
    Nobody ever looks at me twice.

Instrumental 2 | **Am** | **G**   **Em7** | **Am** | **G**   **Em7** ‖

Verse 4

     Am   G Em7
  I'm just a country mile behind
    Am   G Em7
  The world.
     Am   G Em7
  I'm just a country mile behind
    Am   G Em7
  The whole world._____
  Am G Em7
  Oh oh, oh.
  Am G Em7
  Oh oh, oh.
  Am G Em7
  Oh oh, oh. Oh oh, oh.
  Am G Em7
  Oh oh, oh.

Instrumental 3 | Am | G   Em7 | Am | G   Em7 ||

Verse 5

     Am   G Em7
  I'm just a country mile behind
    Am   G Em7
  The world.
     Am   G Em7
  I'm just a country mile behind
    Am G Em7
  The whole world.
  Am G Em7
  Oh oh, oh.
  Am G Em7
  Oh oh, oh.
  Am G Em7
  Oh oh, oh. Oh oh, oh.
  Am G Em7
  Oh oh, oh.

Coda ||: Am | G   Em7 | Am | G   Em7 :||
                           Play 7 times w/vocal ad lib.

    Am G Em7
  I need advice,
    A
  I need advice

Never Had No One Ever

Words & Music by
Morrissey & Johnny Marr

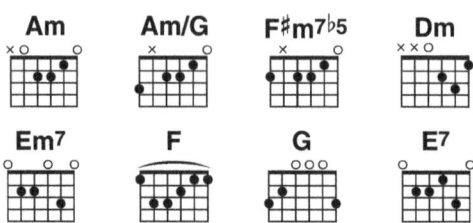

Verse 1

      C Am   Am/G F♯m7♭5   Am
      When you walk without   ease,
Dm Em7 Am   Am/G   F♯m7♭5   Am
On these   streets where you were raised
F   G   Am   Am/G F♯m7♭5   Am
  I   had a really bad dream
Dm Em7 Am   Am/G F♯m7♭5   Am
     It lasted twenty years, seven months, and twenty-seven days.
      F   G
And I know that, I know that
   F   E7   Am Am/G F♯m7♭5 Am Dm Em7
I never ever_____   had no one   ever.

Verse 2

   Am   Am/G F♯m7♭5 Am
     Now I'm outside your   house
F   G   Am
I'm a - lone.
          Am/G F♯m7♭5   Am
And I'm outside your   house
F G   Am   Am/G F♯m7♭5 E7
  I hate to_____ in - trude.
F G   Am   Am/G F♯m7♭5
Oh, I know I'm alone,
        Am
I'm alone, I'm alone, I'm alone
       F   E7   Am/G F♯m7♭5 Am
And I never, ever_____ had no one,   ever
Dm Em7 Am   Am/G F♯m7♭5   Am F G
   I   never had_____ no one,   ever.

© Copyright 1986 Marr Songs Limited/Artane Music Incorporated.
Chrysalis Music Limited (50%)/Universal Music Publishing Limited (50%).
All Rights Reserved. International Copyright Secured.

Chorus
w/vocal ad lib.

Am	Am/G F♯m7♭5	Am	F G
Am	Am/G F♯m7♭5	Am	Dm Em7
Am	Am/G F♯m7♭5	Am	F G
F	F	E7	E7
Am	Am/G F♯m7♭5	Am	Dm Em7 ‖

Coda

‖: Am | Am/G F♯m7♭5 | Am | F   G |
Am	Am/G F♯m7♭5	Am	Dm Em7
Am	Am/G F♯m7♭5	Am	F G
Am	Am/G F♯m7♭5	Am	Dm Em7
Am	Am/G F♯m7♭5	Am	F G
F	F	E7	E7
Am	Am/G F♯m7♭5	Am	Dm Em7 :‖

Repeat to fade

97

Nowhere Fast

Words & Music by
Morrissey & Johnny Marr

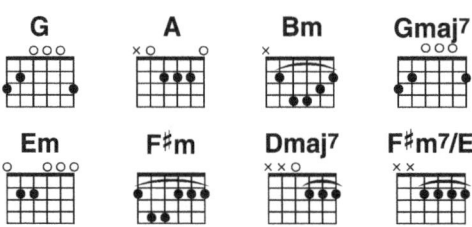

|Intro| | G | A ||

|Verse 1|
    Bm
  I'd like to drop my trousers to the world.
            Gmaj7   **A**
  I am a man of means, of slender means.
    Bm
  Each household appliance
          Em **Gmaj7** **A**
  Is like a new science in my town.

|Chorus 1|
    Bm
  And if the day came when I felt a natural emotion,
  Em   **Gmaj7**
  I'd get such a shock I'd probably jump in the ocean,
    A   **Bm**
  And when a train goes by it's such a sad sound.
  Gmaj7
  No...
  A   **Bm**
    It's such a sad thing.

| Gmaj7 | Gmaj7 | Gmaj7 | Gmaj7 |

| Em | Em | G | A ||

© Copyright 1985 Marr Songs Limited/Artane Music Incorporated.
Chrysalis Music Limited (50%)/Universal Music Publishing Limited (50%).
All Rights Reserved. International Copyright Secured.

Verse 2
        Bm
I'd like to drop my trousers to the queen,
   Em   **Gmaj7**   **A**
Every sensible child will know what this means.
   Bm
The poor and the needy
                    Em   **Gmaj7** **A**
Are selfish and greedy on her terms.

Chorus 2   As Chorus 1

Instrumental | F♯m | F♯m | F♯m | F♯m |
                    | Dmaj7 | Dmaj7 | F♯m7/E | F♯m7/E |
                    | F♯m | F♯m | F♯m | F♯m |
                    | Em | Em | G | A ||

Bridge
                   Bm
And when I'm lying in my bed
   Em   **Gmaj7** **A**
I think about life and I think about death,
   Bm   **Em**   **Gmaj7** **A**
And neither one particularly appeals to me.

Chorus 3
               Bm
And if the day came when I felt a natural emotion
   Em   **Gmaj7** **A**
I'd get such a shock I'd probably lie
   Em   **Gmaj7** **A**
In the middle of the street and die,
   Em   **G**   **A**   **Bm**
I'd lie   down and die,
A **G**
Oh, oh.

Paint A Vulgar Picture

Words & Music by
Morrissey & Johnny Marr

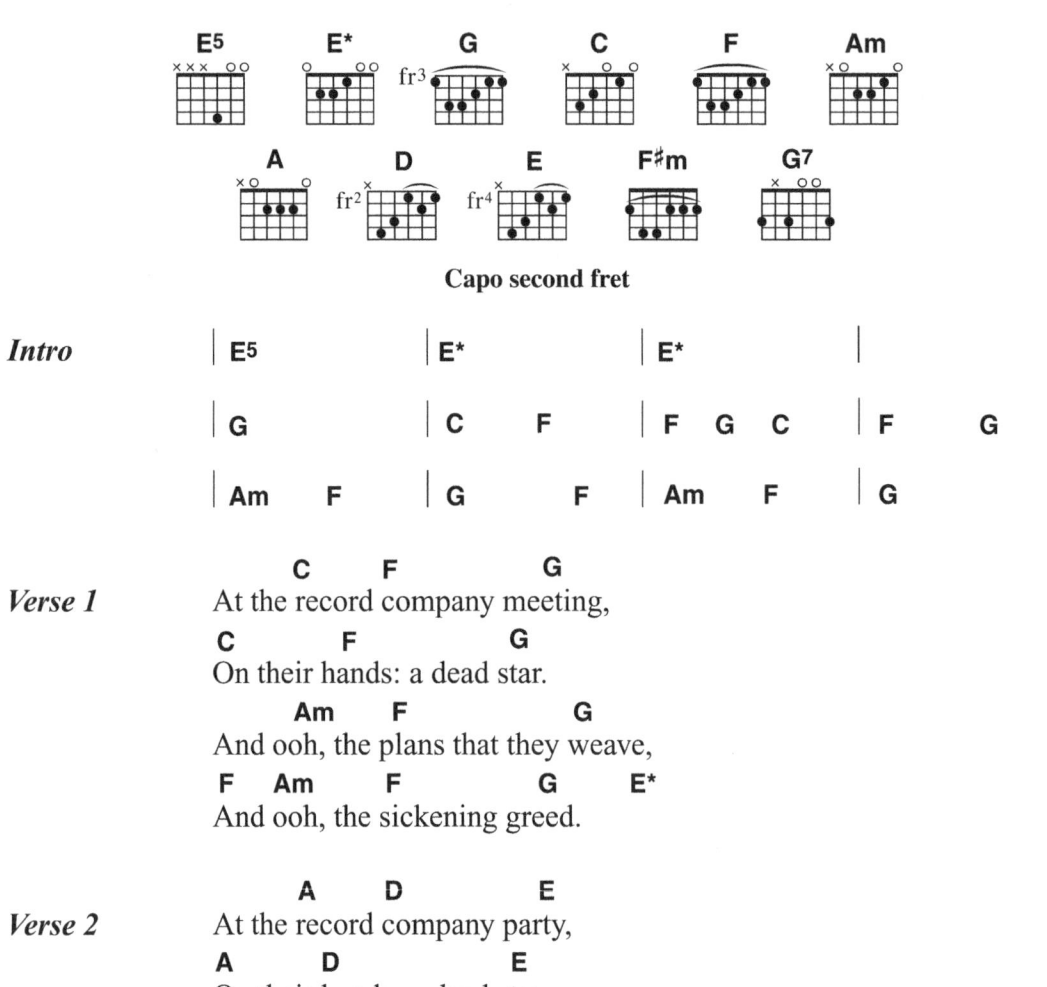

Capo second fret

Intro | E5 | E* | E* | |
    | G | C   F | F   G   C | F   G ||
    | Am   F | G   F | Am   F | G ||

Verse 1
       C   F   G
At the record company meeting,
C   F   G
On their hands: a dead star.
      Am   F   G
And ooh, the plans that they weave,
F   Am   F   G   E*
And ooh, the sickening greed.

Verse 2
     A   D   E
At the record company party,
A   D   E
On their hands: a dead star.
    F#m   D   E
The sycophantic slags all say:

© Copyright 1987 Marr Songs Limited/Artane Music Incorporated.
Chrysalis Music Limited (50%)/Universal Music Publishing Limited (50%).
All Rights Reserved. International Copyright Secured.

	D　　　A　　　D　　　　　E
Verse 2 (cont.)	"I knew him first, and I knew him well."

　　　　　　　　A　　　　D　　　　　　E
　　　　　　　Re-issue! Re-package! Re-package!
　　　　　　　A　D　　E
　　　　　　　Re-evaluate the songs,
　　　　　　　F♯m　　D　　　　　E
　　　　　　　Double pack with a photograph,
　　　　　　　D　　A　　　　　　D　　E　　　　G
　　　　　　　Extra track (and a tacky badge.)

	C　　　　　F
Verse 3	A-list, playlist,

　　　　　　　　　　　　　　　　G
　　　　　　　"Please them, please them, please them!"
　　　　　　　C　　　F　　　　G
　　　　　　　(Sadly, this was your life)
　　　　　　　　　　Am　　　　　　F　　　G
　　　　　　　But you could have said no, if you'd wanted to,
　　　　　　　F　　Am　　　　　　F　　　　G
　　　　　　　　You could have said no, if you'd wanted to.

	C　　　　F
Verse 4	BPI, MTV, BBC,

　　　　　　　　　　　G
　　　　　　　"Please them, please them!"
　　　　　　　C　　　F　　　　G
　　　　　　　(Sadly, this was your life)
　　　　　　　　　　Am　　　　　　F　　　G
　　　　　　　But you could have said no, if you'd wanted to,
　　　　　　　F　　Am　　　　F　　　　　G　　　　　　　　　　　E*
　　　　　　　You could have walked away, couldn't you?

	A　　　D　　　　　　　　　E
Verse 5	I touched you at the soundcheck,

　　　　　　　　　　A　　　D　　　E
　　　　　　　You had no real way of knowing.
　　　　　　　　　　F♯m　　D　　　　　　　　E　　　　　　D
　　　　　　　In my heart I begged, "Take me with you.
　　　　　　　　F♯m　　　D　　　　　E
　　　　　　　I don't care where you're going."

Verse 6

    A   **D**
But to you I was faceless,
     E
I was fawning, I was boring.
   A   **D**   **E**
A child from those ugly new houses,
    F#m **D** **E**
Who could never begin to know,
D   **F#m D** **E** **G**
Who could never really know.

Instrumental | C F | F G C | F   G | Am F |
          | G   F | Am F | G | C   F |
          | F G C | F   G | Am F | F G F |
          | Am F | G | E* ||

Verse 7

   A   **D**   **E**
Best of! Most of! Satiate the need,
 A   **D**   **E**
Slip them into different sleeves!
  F#m **D**   **E** **D**
Buy both, and feel deceived,
F#m   **D**   **E**
Climber, new entry, re-entry.

Verse 8

   A   **D**
World tour! ("Media whore!")
     E   **A**
"Please the press in Belgium!"
 D   **E**
(This was your life...)
       F#m **D**   **E**   **D**
And when it fails to recoup? Well, maybe:
  F#m   **D**   **E** **G**
You just haven't earned it yet, baby.

Verse 9

         C   F   G
I walked a pace behind you at the soundcheck,
     C   F   G
You're just the same as I am.
 Am   F   G
What makes most people feel happy
F   Am   F   G
Leads us headlong into harm.
        C   F
So, in my bedroom in those ugly new houses,
 G   C   F   G
I danced my legs down to the knees.
     Am F   G   F   Am   F   G   E*
But me and my true love will never meet again...

Verse 10

     A   D   E
At the record company meeting,
        A   D   E
On their hands, at last, a dead star!
          F♯m D   E
But they can never taint you in my eyes,
D   F♯m D   E
They can never touch you now.
     A   D   E
No, they cannot hurt you my darling,
    A   D   E
They cannot touch you now,
 F♯m D   E   D F♯m D   E
But me and my true love will never meet again.

Coda

‖: G7 | G7 | G7 | G7 :‖

Repeat to fade

Panic

Words & Music by
Morrissey & Johnny Marr

[Chord diagrams: C, D, F, G, Em, E, A5, B5, C#5 (fr 4), D5 (fr 5)]

Intro | C | D   F   C ||

Verse
    G   Em
Panic on the streets of London,
    G   Em
Panic on the streets of Birmingham,
  C   G   D   F C
I wonder to myself.
  G   Em
Could life ever be sane again?
        G   Em
The Leeds side-streets that you slip down.
  C   G   D   F C
I wonder to myself…
G   Em
Hopes may rise on the Grasmere,
  G   Em
   But Honey Pie, you're not safe here,
          C   G   D   F C
So you run down to the safety of the town.
        G   Em
But there's Panic on the streets of Carlisle,
G   Em
Dublin, Dundee, Humberside,
  C   G   D   F C
I wonder to myself…

Instrumental 1 | E | E   A5 B5 | C#5 | D5 |

                       | E | E   A5 B5 | C#5 | D5 ||

© Copyright 1986 Marr Songs Limited/Artane Music Incorporated.
Chrysalis Music Limited (50%)/Universal Music Publishing Limited (50%).
All Rights Reserved. International Copyright Secured.

Chorus

```
        G              Em
Burn down the disco,
   G            Em
Hang the blessed DJ,
          C           G         D
Because the music that they constantly play,
       G              Em
It says nothing to me about my life.
   G            Em
Hang the blessed DJ,
          C         G         D
Because the music they constantly play
F  C    G                      Em
   On the Leeds side-streets that you slip down,
      G             Em
Provincial towns you jog 'round....
         C           G           D
Hang the DJ, hang the DJ, hang the DJ,
         C           G           D
Hang the DJ, hang the DJ, hang the DJ.
         C           G           D
Hang the DJ, hang the DJ, hang the DJ,
F    C   G               Em
Hang the DJ, hang the DJ,
            G             Em
Hang the DJ, hang the DJ.
         C           G           D
Hang the DJ, hang the DJ, hang the DJ,
F    C   G               Em
Hang the DJ, hang the DJ,
            G             Em
Hang the DJ, hang the DJ.
         C           G           D
Hang the DJ, hang the DJ, Hang the DJ,

Hang the DJ, hang the DJ,
F    C   G               Em
Hang the DJ, hang the DJ.
            G             Em
Hang the DJ, hang the DJ, hang the DJ...    ad lib. to fade
```

Please, Please, Please, Let Me Get What I Want

Words & Music by
Morrissey & Johnny Marr

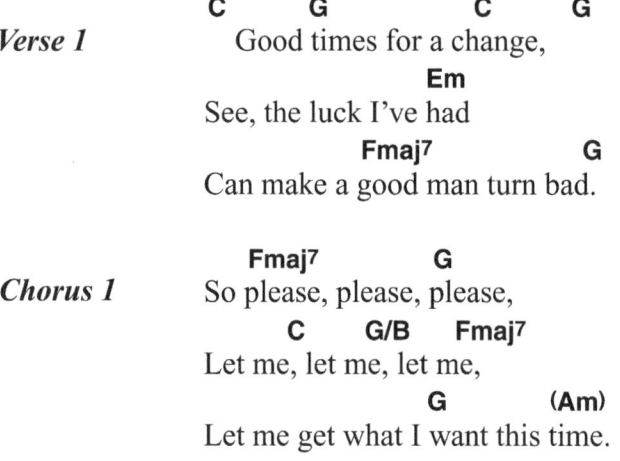

Capo second fret

Verse 1
```
         C     G          C     G
      Good times for a change,
                  Em
      See, the luck I've had
                Fmaj7         G
      Can make a good man turn bad.
```

Chorus 1
```
         Fmaj7        G
      So please, please, please,
              C    G/B    Fmaj7
      Let me, let me, let me,
                    G       (Am)
      Let me get what I want this time.
```

Instrumental | Am | Am | Fmaj7 | G ||

Verse 2
```
         C            G           C     G
      Haven't had a dream in a long time
                  Em
      See, the life I've had
                Fmaj7       G
      Can make a good man bad.
```

© Copyright 1984 Warner/Chappell Music Limited (50%)/Copyright Control (50%).
All Rights Reserved. International Copyright Secured.

Chorus 2

        Fmaj7   **G**
So for once in my life,
         C **G/B**   **Fmaj7**
Let me   get what I want.
            G   **Am**
Lord knows it would be the first time,
Fmaj7   **G**   **C**   **C9**
Lord knows it would be the first time.

Coda

Fmaj7	G	C G/B	Fmaj7
Fmaj7	G	C	C9
Em	Em	Am	Am
Fmaj7	Fmaj7	G 𝄐	‖

Pretty Girls Make Graves

Words & Music by
Morrissey & Johnny Marr

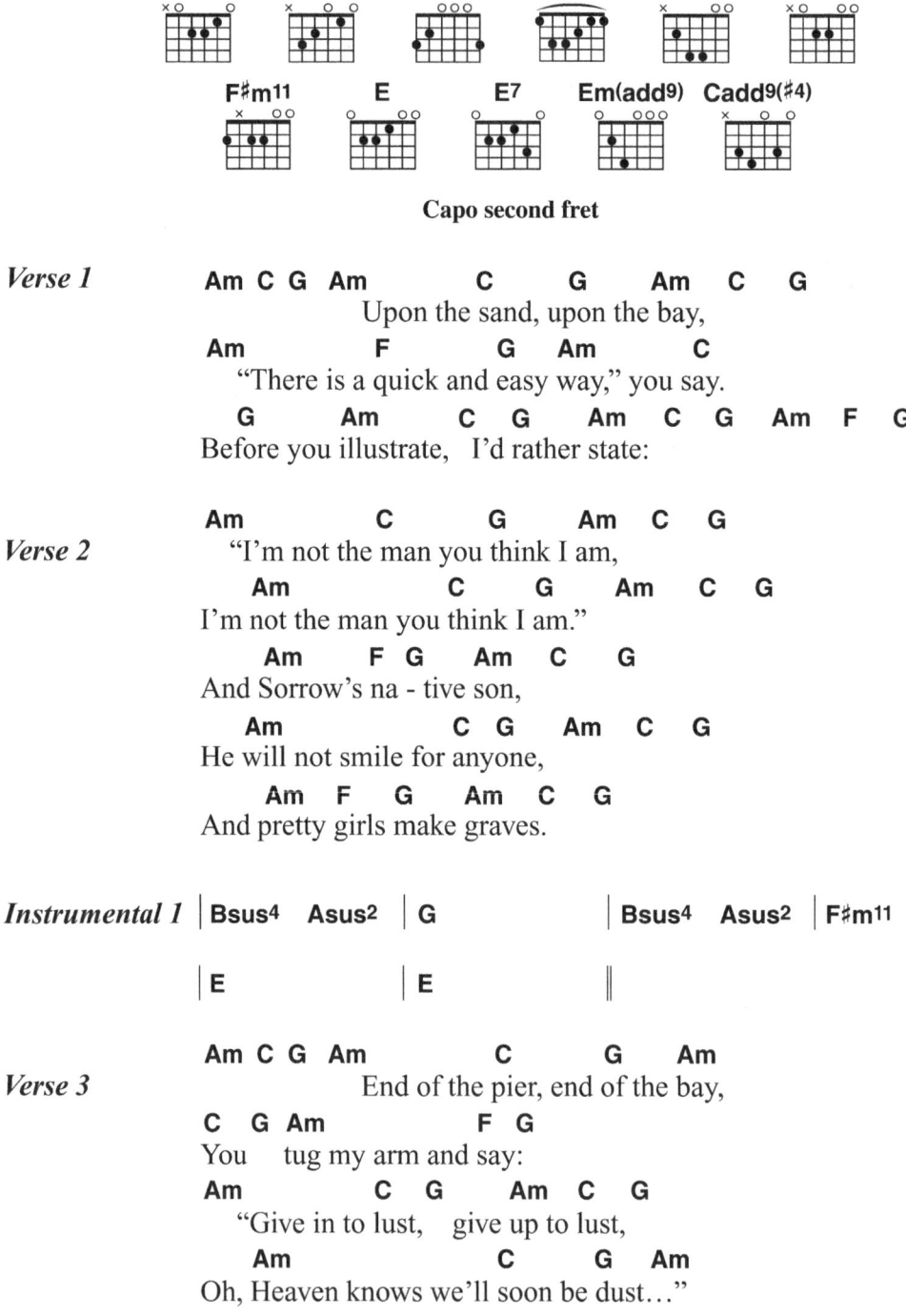

Capo second fret

Verse 1
```
        Am C G Am         C       G      Am  C  G
              Upon the sand, upon the bay,
        Am          F        G    Am       C
        "There is a quick and easy way," you say.
         G      Am      C G   Am   C G  Am  F  G
        Before you illustrate, I'd rather state:
```

Verse 2
```
        Am         C        G    Am  C  G
        "I'm not the man you think I am,
         Am         C        G    Am  C  G
        I'm not the man you think I am."
         Am      F   G   Am   C   G
        And Sorrow's na - tive son,
         Am           C  G   Am   C  G
        He will not smile for anyone,
         Am     F   G    Am   C   G
        And pretty girls make graves.
```

Instrumental 1 | Bsus4 Asus2 | G | Bsus4 Asus2 | F#m11 |
                  | E | E   ‖

Verse 3
```
        Am C G Am         C      G     Am
              End of the pier, end of the bay,
        C  G Am          F   G
        You   tug my arm and say:
        Am           C   G    Am   C  G
        "Give in to lust, give up to lust,
        Am              C      G   Am
        Oh, Heaven knows we'll soon be dust…"
```

© Copyright 1984 Marr Songs Limited/Artane Music Incorporated.
Chrysalis Music Limited (50%)/Universal Music Publishing Limited (50%).
All Rights Reserved. International Copyright Secured.

Verse 4

           F G Am   **C**   **G**   **Am C G**
"Oh,   I'm not the man you think I am,
              Am   **C**   **G**   **Am C G**
I'm not the man you think I am."
              Am   **F G**   **Am C G**
And sorrow's na - tive son,
          Am   **C G**   **Am C G**
He will not rise for anyone,
         Am   **F** **G**   **Am C G**
And pretty girls make graves.

Instrumental 2 As Instrumental 1

Verse 5

        Am C G **Am**   **C**   **G** **Am**
   I   could have been wild and I could have been free,
    C G Am   **F**   **G**   **Am**
But nature played this trick on me.
         C   **G**
She wants it now,
      Am   **C**   **G** **Am**
  And she will not wait,
        F   **G**   **Am**   **C G**
But she's too rough and I'm too delicate.
        Am   **C**   **G** **Am**
  Then on the sand, another man,
        C   **G**   **Am**
  He takes her hand,
        C   **G**   **Am**   **F**   **G**   **Am**
A smile   lights up her stupid face (and well it would).
    C G Am   **C**   **G**
I   lost my faith in womanhood,
      Am   **C**   **G**
I lost my faith in womanhood,
      Am   **F G**   **Am** **C G**
I lost my faith.

Coda

| **Bsus4** **Asus2** | **G** | **Bsus4** **Asus2** | **F♯m11** |
| **E** | **E** | | |

‖: **E7** | **E7** | **E7** | **E7** :‖
                                             Play 4 times

‖: **Em(add9)** | **Cadd9(♯4)** | **Em(add9)** | **Cadd9(♯4)** :‖
                                         Repeat to fade

The Queen Is Dead

Words & Music by
Morrissey & Johnny Marr

Intro ‖ Drums ‖

| G5 | A5 | E/G♯ | G5 ‖

Verse 1
                B5
Farewell to this land's cheerless marches,

Hemmed in like a boar between arches.

Her very lowness with her head in a sling,
                       D5   E5
I'm truly sorry, but it sounds like a wonderful thing.

Verse 2
         B5
     I say, Charles don't you ever crave

To appear on the front of the Daily Mail,
    D5   E5
Dressed in your mother's bridal veil?

Instrumental 1 | G5 | A5 | E/G♯ | G5 ‖

Verse 3
         B5
And so I checked all the registered historical facts,

And I was shocked into shame to discover

How I'm the eigteenth pale descendant
         D5   E5
Of some old queen or other.

© Copyright 1986 Marr Songs Limited/Artane Music Incorporated.
Chrysalis Music Limited (50%)/Universal Music Publishing Limited (50%).
All Rights Reserved. International Copyright Secured.

Verse 4

    B5
Oh, has the world changed, or have I changed?

Oh, has the world changed, or have I changed?

Some nine year old tough who peddles drugs
                 D5   **E5**
I swear to God, I swear I never even knew what drugs were.

Instrumental 2 | G5 | A5 | E/G♯ | G5   ‖

Verse 5

    B5
So I broke into the palace

With a sponge and a rusty spanner

She said: "Eh, I know you, and you cannot sing."
                     D5   **E5**
I said: "That's nothing: you should hear me play piano."

Verse 6

    B5
We can go for a walk where it's quiet and dry

And talk about precious things

But when you are tied to your mother's apron
D5   **E5**
No-one talks about castration.

Instrumental 3 | G5 | A5 | E/G♯ | G5   ‖

Verse 7

    B5
We can go for a walk where it's quiet and dry

And talk about precious things

Like love and law and poverty
D5   **E5**
These are the things that kill me.

Verse 8

          B5
We can go for a walk where it's quiet and dry

And talk about precious things,

But the rain that flattens my hair, oh,
D5   **E5**
These are the things that kill me.

Instrumental 4 | **G5** | **A5** | **E/G♯** | **G5** |

                | **B5** | **B5** | ‖

Verse 9

    B5
Pass the pub that saps your body,

And the church who'll snatch your money.
         D5
The queen is dead, boys,
    E5
And it's so lonely on a limb.

Verse 10

    B5
Pass the pub that wrecks your body,

And the church, all they want is your money.
        D5
The queen is dead, boys,
    E5
And it's so lonely on a limb.

Instrumental 5 | **G5** | **A5** | **E/G♯** | **G5** |

                | **B5** | **B5** | ‖

Coda

        D5   E5   B5
Life is very long, when you're lonely,
        D5   E5   B5
Life is very long, when you're lonely,
        D5   E5   B5
Life is very long, when you're lonely,
        D5   E5   B5
Life is very long, when you're lonely.

‖: D5 | E5 | B | B |

| B | B   :‖   *Repeat ad lib. to fade*

Reel Around The Fountain

Words & Music by
Morrissey & Johnny Marr

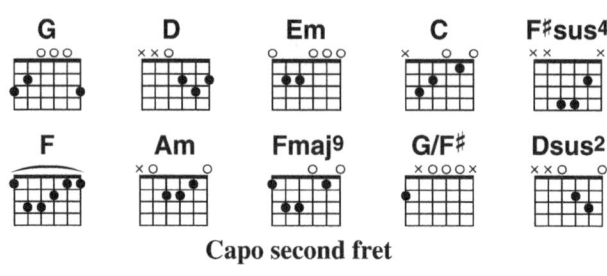

Capo second fret

Intro ‖   Drums   ‖

Verse 1
      G
It's time the tale were told,
  D
Of how you took a child
     Em   C G
And you made him old.

It's time the tale were told,
  D
Of how you took a child
           Em
And you made him old,
C   G   F♯sus4
You made him old.

Pre-Chorus 1
  F   Em
Reel around the fountain
Am
Slap me on the patio
   Fmaj9 Em D
I'll take it now.

Chorus 1
  G   D
Fifteen minutes with you,
  G   D C
Well, I wouldn't say no.
  G   G/F♯
Oh people said that you were virtually dead,
  C   D
And they were so wrong!

© Copyright 1984 Marr Songs Limited/Artane Music Incorporated.
Chrysalis Music Limited (50%)/Universal Music Publishing Limited (50%).
All Rights Reserved. International Copyright Secured.

Chorus 2

```
        G                    D
Fifteen minutes with you,
        G          D   C
Oh I wouldn't say no.
        G                  G/F♯
Oh people said that you were easily led
                C         Am
And they were half-right,

And they were half-right…
```

Instrumental 1 ‖: C | C | Am | Am :‖

| C | Dsus2 | ‖

Verse 2 As Verse 1

Pre-Chorus 2 As Pre-Chorus 1

Chorus 3

```
        G                    D
Fifteen minutes with you,
        G          D   C
Oh I wouldn't say no.
        G          G/F♯
Oh people see no worth in you,
          C    Am
I do,
```

Chorus 4 As Chorus 3

Instrumental 2 As Instrumental 1

Verse 3 I dreamt about you last night,
                  D
              And I fell out of bed twice.
                    Em   **C**   **G**
              You can pin and mount me like a butterfly,

              But "Take me to the haven of your bed,"
                 D
              Was something that you never said.
                Em   **C**
              Two lumps, please, you're the bee's knees,
                  G   **F♯sus4**
              But so am I.

                F   **Em**
Pre-Chorus 3 Meet me at the fountain,
              Am
              Shove me on the patio,
                   Fmaj9   **Em**   **D**
              I'll take it slowly.

Chorus 5   As Chorus 3

Chorus 6   As Chorus 3

Coda   ‖: C | C | Am | Am :‖
w/vocal ad lib.
               | C | Dsus2 | G ‖

Rubber Ring

Words & Music by
Morrissey & Johnny Marr

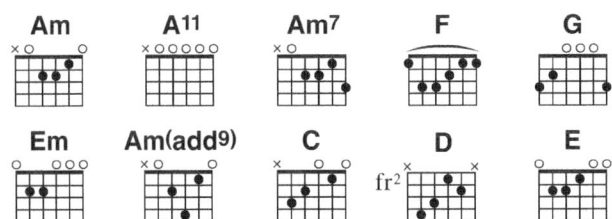

Capo seventh fret

Intro | Am | Am   A11 | Am | Am   Am7 |
       | Am | Am   A11 | Am | Am |
       | Am | Am ||

Verse 1
```
            F           G     Am
A sad fact widely known:
                  Am
The most impassionate song

To a lonely soul
           F           G    Am
Is so easily outgrown.
```

Verse 2
```
But don't forget the songs

That made you smile,
           F              G    Am
And the songs that made you cry.

When you lay in awe on the bedroom floor,
               F              G     Am
And said: "Oh, oh, smother me, mother…"
```

© Copyright 1987 Marr Songs Limited/Artane Music Incorporated.
Chrysalis Music Limited (50%)/Universal Music Publishing Limited (50%).
All Rights Reserved. International Copyright Secured.

Chorus 1
      F Em
Oh, oh,
          F   Em
La-de-day, la-de-day
          F   G   Am
La-de-day, la-de-day,
     F   Em
Oh, na, na, na,
         F   Em
La-de-day, la-de-day,
         F   G   Am
La-de-day.
F   Em
Oh, oh,
F   Em
Laddle-la-day, laddle-la-day
F   G   Am
Laddle-la-day.

Verse 3
       (Am)
The passing of time,

And all it's crimes
 F   G   Am
Is making me sad again.

The passing of time,
                                  F   G   Am
And all of its sickening crimes is making me sad again.

Verse 4
       (Am)
But don't forget the songs that made you cry,
   F   G   Am
And the songs that saved your life,

Yes, you're older now and you're a clever swine
                F   G   Am
But they were the only ones who ever stood by you.

Instrumental ‖: F | Em | F Em | F G Am :‖
                                                                     Play 3 times

Verse 5

    (Am)
The passing of time leaves empty lives,
F   **G**   **Am**
Waiting to be filled.

The passing of time leaves empty lives,
F   **G**   **Am**
Waiting to be filled.

Verse 6

I'm here with the cause,

I'm holding the torch.
    F   **G** **Am**
In the corner of the room, can you hear me?

And when you're dancing and laughing,

And finally living,
   F   **G** **Am**
Here my voice in your head and think of me kindly.

Chorus 2   As Chorus 1

Coda

Am **Am(add9)** **C**   **D**
Do   you   love me like you used to?

| **E** | **F** **C** | |

||: **F** | **Em** | **F** **Em** | **F** **G** **Am** :||

Repeat w/vocal ad lib. to fade

A Rush And A Push And The Land Is Ours

Words & Music by
Morrissey & Johnny Marr

Dm   B♭   Am/C   E♭   C   E♭maj7

Intro

| Dm | B♭   Am/C ||

Verse 1

    Dm   B♭   Am/C   Dm
I am the ghost of Troubled Joe,
        B♭   Am/C
Hung by his pretty white neck
Dm
Some eighteen months ago.
B♭   Am/C Dm   B♭
   I travelled to a   mystical time zone,
        Am/C Dm   B♭
And I missed my   bed and I soon came home.

Verse 2

                     Dm
They said: "There's too much caffeine
       B♭
In your blood stream,
Am/C Dm   B♭
And a lack of real spice in your life."
               Am/C Dm   B♭
I said: "Leave me a - lone because I'm alright, dad,
Am/C Dm   B♭
Just surprised to still be on my own…"

Pre-Chorus

    E♭   Dm
Ooh, but don't mention love,
      E♭   Dm   B♭ C
I'd hate the strain of the pain again.

© Copyright 1987 Marr Songs Limited/Artane Music Incorporated.
Chrysalis Music Limited (50%)/Universal Music Publishing Limited (50%).
All Rights Reserved. International Copyright Secured.

Chorus 1

     Dm   B♭   Am/C Dm
A rush and a push and the land that we stand on   is   ours,
               B♭   Am/C   Dm
It has been before so it shall be a - gain.
               B♭   Am/C   Dm
And people who are uglier than you and   I,
            B♭   Am/C
They take what they need, and just leave.
E♭   Dm
Ooh, but don't mention love,
         E♭   Dm   B♭ C
I'd hate the pain of the strain all over again.

Chorus 2

     Dm   B♭   Am/C Dm
A rush and a push and the land that we stand on is   ours,
              B♭   Am/C   Dm
It has been before so why can't it be   now?
               B♭   Am/C   Dm
And people who are weaker than you and   I,
           B♭   Am/C
They take what they want from life.
E♭   Dm
Ooh, but don't mention love,
E♭   Dm   B♭ C
No: just don't mention love!

Chorus 3

     Dm   B♭   Am/C Dm
A rush and a push and the land we stand on is   ours,
            B♭   Am/C Dm
Your youth may be gone but you're still a good man.
             B♭
So phone me, phone me,
Am/C Dm   B♭   Am/C
So   phone me, phone me, phone me.
E♭maj7   Dm
Ooh, I think I'm in love,
E♭maj7   Dm
Ooh, I think I'm in love.
E♭maj7   Dm
Ooh, I think I'm in love,
E♭maj7   Dm
Urrgh, I think I'm in lerv.

Coda

‖: E♭maj7 | Dm | E♭maj7 | Dm :‖

Repeat to fade

Rusholme Ruffians

Words & Music by
Morrissey & Johnny Marr

C   Am   G   F#   F

Capo second fret

Intro

C	C	
C	C	C G	F# F
C Am	C Am	C Am	

Verse 1

    G F#   F   C
    The last night of the fair,
Am   C   Am
By the big wheel generator
  C
A boy is stabbed
     Am
And his money is grabbed,
G   F#   F | C   Am |
And the air hangs heavy like a dulling wine.
       C   Am
She is famous, she is funny,
   C
An engagement ring
     Am
Doesn't mean a thing
G   F#   F
To a mind consumed by brass (money).

| C Am | C Am | C Am ||

Chorus 1

```
      G  F#   F                    C
And though I   walk home alone,
      Am          C        Am   |C         Am    |
I might walk home alone,
G              F#    F
But my faith in love is still devout.

     |C         Am    |C        Am    |C        Am    |
```

Verse 2

```
      G  F#     F              C
        The last night of the fair,
Am                C         Am
From a seat on a   whirling waltzer,
         C            Am
Her skirt ascends for a watching eye.
G         F#      F                         C
It's a hideous trait (on her mother's side),
Am                C         Am
From a seat on a   whirling waltzer,
         C            Am
Her skirt ascends for a watching eye.
G         F#      F
It's a hideous trait (on her mother's side).

     |C         Am    |C        Am    |C        Am    |
```

Chorus 2   As Chorus 1

Verse 3

```
      G        F# F   C
        Then someone falls in love,
Am              C        Am
And someone's beaten up,
          C        Am
Someone's beaten up,
G        F#        F                      C
And the senses being dulled are mine.
Am           C
And someone falls in love,
Am              C        Am
And someone's beaten up,
G        F#       F
And the senses being dulled are mine.

     |C         Am    |C        Am    |C        Am    |
```

123

Chorus 3   As Chorus 1

Verse 4
    G F♯   F   **C**
This is the last night of the fair
Am   **C**
And the grease in the hair
      Am   **C**   **Am**
Of a speedway operator
G   **F♯**   **F**
Is all a tremulous heart requires,
C   **Am**   **C**
   A schoolgirl is denied,
Am   **C**   **Am**
   She said, "How quickly would I die
G   **F♯**   **F**
If I jumped from the top of the parachute?"

|**C**   **Am** |**C**   **Am** |**C**   **Am** |

Verse 5   As Verse 4

Verse 6
    G F♯ F   **C**   **Am**   **C**   **Am**
   So,   scratch my name on your arm with a fountain pen,
C   **Am G**   **F**   **C**
   (This means you really love me).
                          Am   **C**   **Am**
Scratch my name on your arm with a fountain pen,
C   **Am G**   **F**   **C**
   (This means you really love me).

|**C**   **Am** |**C**   **Am** |**C**   **Am** |
Oh...

Chorus 4

```
       G  F#    F                      C
       And though I    walk home alone,
           Am         C         Am  | C          Am    |
       I just might walk home alone,
       G         F#    F
       But my faith in love is still devout.
         C    Am        C         Am  | C          Am    |
           I might walk home alone,
       G          F#    F
       But my faith in love is still devout.
         C    Am        C         Am  | C          Am    |
           I might walk home alone,
       G          F#    F
       But my faith in love is still devout.

       | C         Am   | C         Am   | C    Am   G   | F#   F        ||
```

Shakespeare's Sister

Words & Music by
Morrissey & Johnny Marr

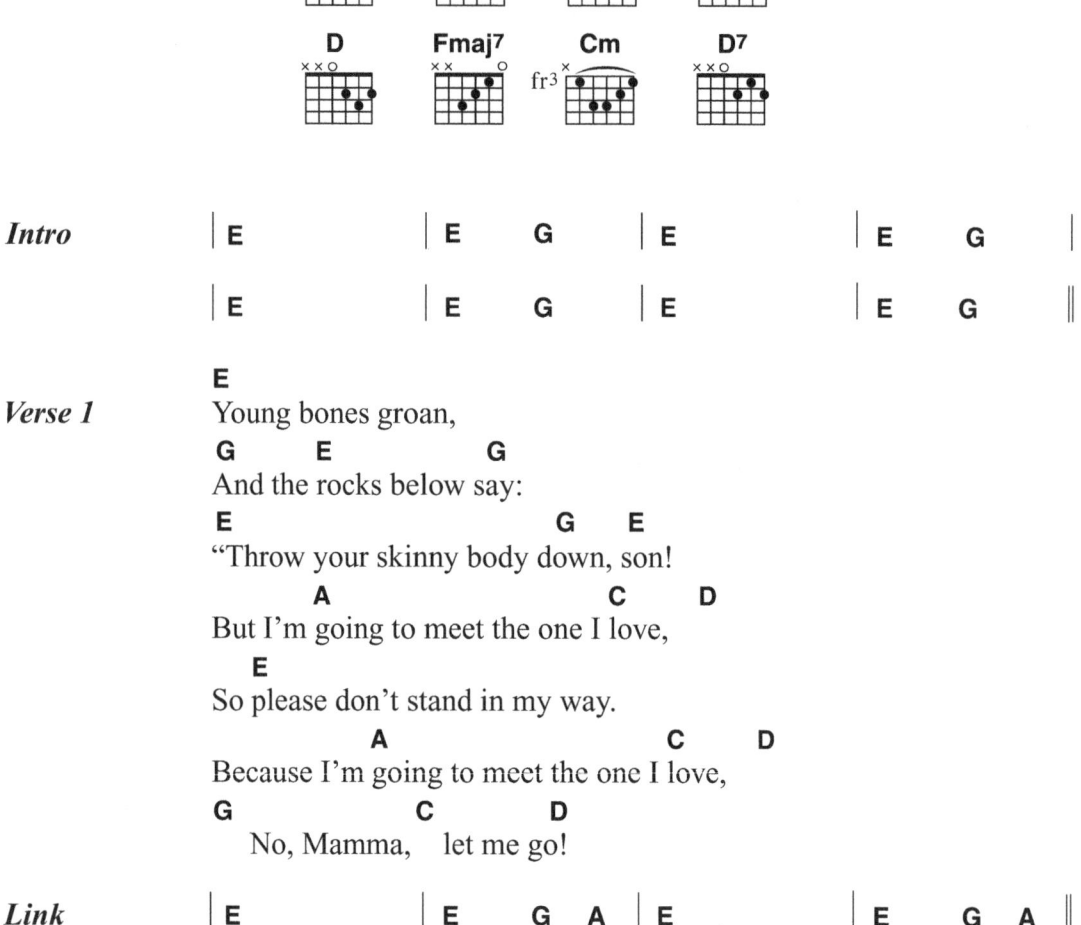

Verse 2

    E
Young bones groan,
  G   E   G
And the rocks below say:
E   G   E
"Throw your white body down!"
          A   C   D
But I'm going to meet the one I love,
    E
At last! At last! At last!
      A   C
I'm going to meet the one I love,
   D
La-de-da, la-de-da,
G   C   D
  No, mamma, let me go!

Instrumental

C	C	Fmaj7	Fmaj7
D	G	D	G
: G	G	Cm	D7
E	E G	E	E G :
E	E G	E	E G
E	E G	||	

Verse 3

  E   A
I thought that if you had an acoustic guitar,
          C   D   E
Then it meant that you were a protest singer.
          A
Oh, I can smile about it now,
      C   D
But at the time it was terrible.
  G   C   D   G
No,_____ mamma, let me go!
C   D   G   C   D
    No, no, no…

Coda

| A | A | C | D | E 𝄐 ||

Sheila Take A Bow

Words & Music by
Morrissey & Johnny Marr

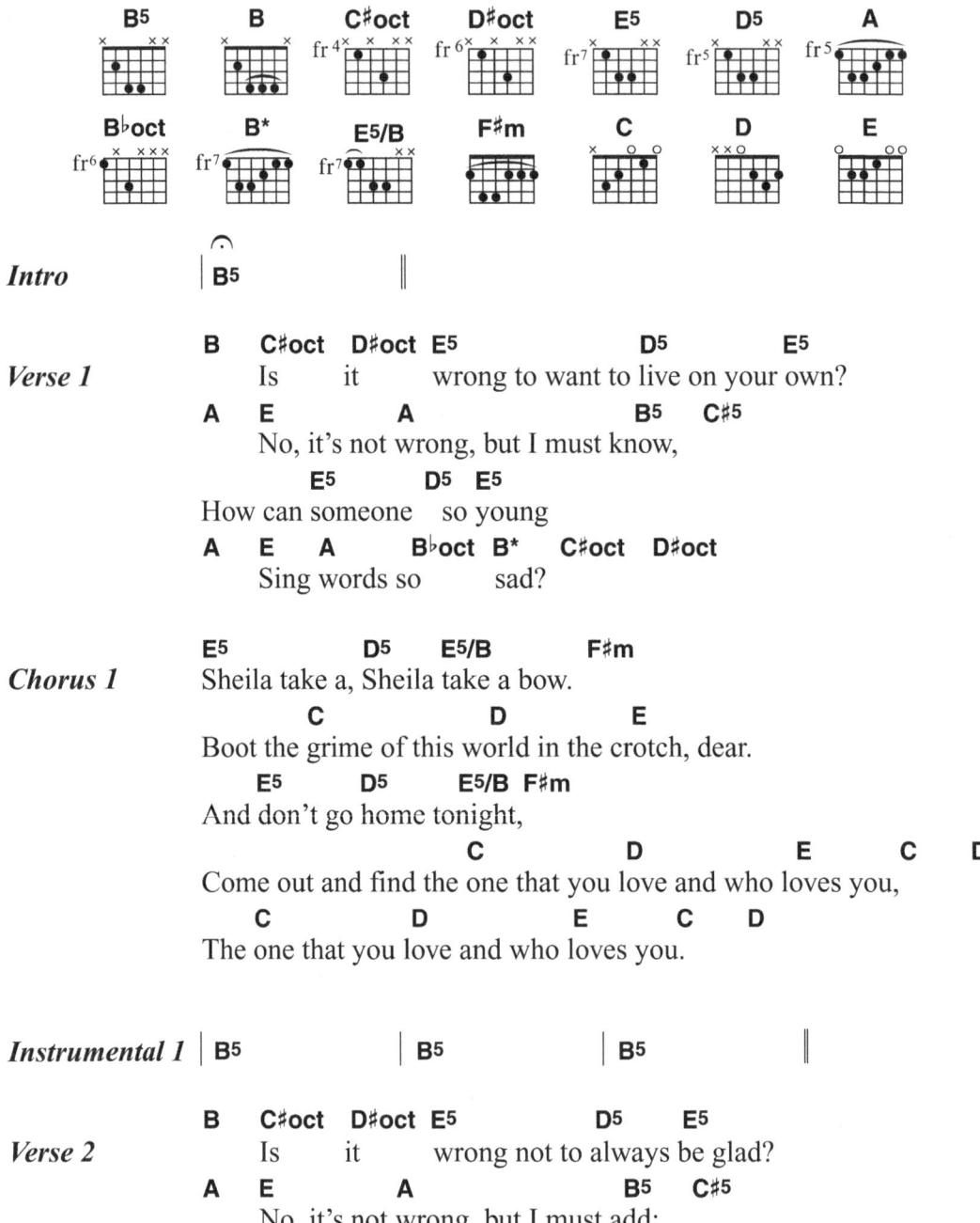

Intro | B5 ||

Verse 1
```
       B   C#oct D#oct E5           D5          E5
       Is   it    wrong to want to live on your own?
       A    E    A                  B5    C#5
       No, it's not wrong, but I must know,
            E5         D5   E5
       How can someone  so young
       A    E    A    Bboct B*   C#oct D#oct
       Sing words so      sad?
```

Chorus 1
```
       E5          D5     E5/B       F#m
       Sheila take a, Sheila take a bow.
            C           D            E
       Boot the grime of this world in the crotch, dear.
       E5          D5    E5/B F#m
       And don't go home tonight,
            C           D          E              C   D
       Come out and find the one that you love and who loves you,
            C           D         E          C   D
       The one that you love and who loves you.
```

Instrumental 1 | B5 | B5 | B5 ||

Verse 2
```
       B   C#oct D#oct E5           D5          E5
       Is   it    wrong not to always be glad?
       A    E    A                  B5    C#5
       No, it's not wrong, but I must add:
```

© Copyright 1987 Marr Songs Limited/Artane Music Incorporated.
Chrysalis Music Limited (50%)/Universal Music Publishing Limited (50%).
All Rights Reserved. International Copyright Secured.

Verse 2 (cont.) How can someone   so young
                        E5   D5 E5

A E A   B♭oct B*   C♯oct D♯oct
Sing words so   sad?

Chorus 2   As Chorus 1

Instrumental 2 | B5 | B5 | B5 | B5 |

                | B5 | B5 | B5   ‖

Chorus 3
B   C♯oct D♯oct E5   D5   E5/B F♯m
    Take   my   hand and off we stride,
C   D   E
Oh, la, la, la, la, la, la, la, la.
         E5   D5   E5/B F♯m
You're a girl and I'm a boy,
C   D   E   C D
La, la, la, la, la, la, la, la.
C   D   E
La, la, la, la, la, la.

Chorus 4
          E5   D5   E5/B F♯m
Take my hand and off we stride,
    C   D   E
Oh, la, la, la, la, la, la, la, la
         E5   D5   E5/B F♯m
I'm a girl and you're a boy,
C   D   E   C D
La, la, la, la, la, la, la, la
C   D   E
La, la, la, la, la, la.

Chorus 5
E5   D5   E5/B   F♯m
Sheila take a, Sheila take a bow.
C   D   E
La, la, la, la, la, la, la, la.
          E5   D5   E5/B F♯m
Throw your homework onto the fire,
     C   D   E   C D
Come out and find the one that you love,
     C   D   E5
Come out and find the one you love.

Shoplifters Of The World Unite

Words & Music by
Morrissey & Johnny Marr

G   E   A   Cmaj7   Am7   Dsus4   D

Verse 1

      G E
          Learn to love me,
                  G A
Assemble the ways,
    E   G A
Now, today, tomorrow and always.
    E   G A
      My only weakness is a listed crime,
    E
      My only weakness is… well, never mind, never mind.

Chorus 1

      G   Cmaj7   Am7   Dsus4 D
      Shoplifters of the world,
      G   Cmaj7   Am7   Dsus4 D
      Unite and take over.
      G   Cmaj7   Am7   Dsus4 D
      Shoplifters of the world,
           G   Cmaj7   Am7
Hand it over, hand it over, hand it over.

Verse 2

      G E
          Learn to love me,
                  G A
And assemble the ways,
    E   G A
Now, today, tomorrow and always.
    E   G A
      My only weakness is a listed crime,
      E
But last night the plans of a future war

Was all I saw on Channel Four.

© Copyright 1986 Marr Songs Limited/Artane Music Incorporated.
Chrysalis Music Limited (50%)/Universal Music Publishing Limited (50%).
All Rights Reserved. International Copyright Secured.

Chorus 2   As Chorus 1

Instrumental   ‖: E | E | E | E   G   A :‖
                                                              Play 4 times

| G | Cmaj7 | Am7   Dsus4 D | G |
| Cmaj7 | Am7   Dsus4 D | G | Cmaj7 |
| Am7   Dsus4 D | G | Cmaj7 | Am7   Dsus4 D ‖

Bridge
   G   Cmaj7   Am7
  A heartless hand on my shoulder,
             Dsus4   D
A push and it's over.
 G   Cmaj7   Am7
  Alabaster crashes down,
       Dsus4   D   G
(Six months is a   long time.)
      Cmaj7   Am7
Tried living in the real world,
   Dsus4   D   G
Instead of a shell,
       Cmaj7 Am7
But before I began…
Dsus4 D   G   Cmaj7   Am7   Dsus4 D
I   was bored before I even began.

Chorus 3
   G   Cmaj7   Am7 Dsus4   D
  Shoplifters of the world,
   G   Cmaj7   Am7 Dsus4   D
  Unite and take over.
   G   Cmaj7   Am7 Dsus4   D
  Shoplifters of the world,
   G   Cmaj7   Am7 Dsus4   D
  Unite and take over.
   G   Cmaj7   Am7 Dsus4   D
  Shoplifters of the world,
   G   Cmaj7   Am7 Dsus4   D
  Unite and take over.
   G   Cmaj7   Am7
  Shoplifters of the world,
Dsus4   D   G
Take   over.

Some Girls Are Bigger Than Others

Words & Music by
Morrissey & Johnny Marr

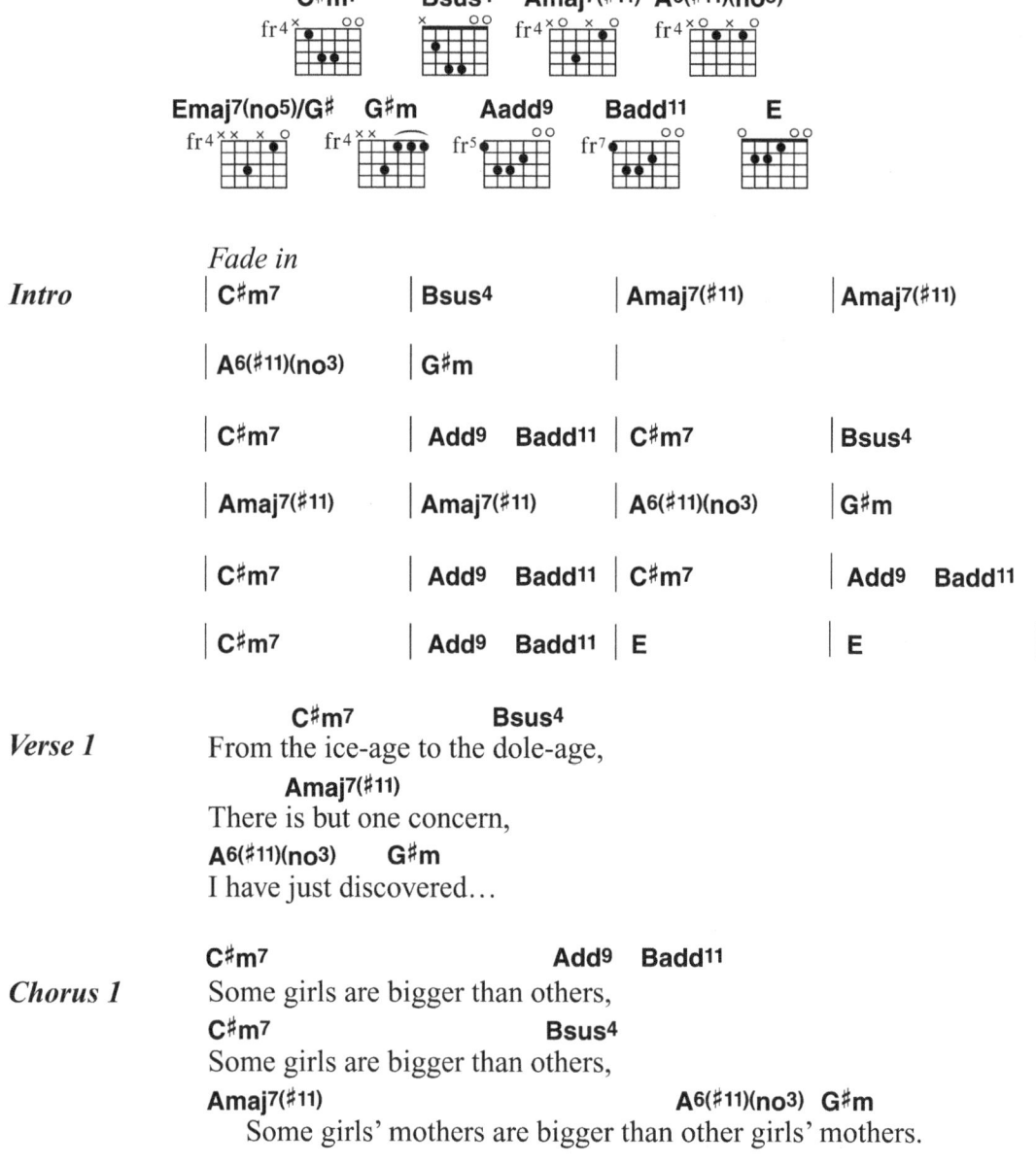

Intro
	Fade in			
	| C#m7	| Bsus4	| Amaj7(#11)	| Amaj7(#11) |
	| A6(#11)(no3)	| G#m		
	| C#m7	| Add9 Badd11	| C#m7	| Bsus4 |
	| Amaj7(#11)	| Amaj7(#11)	| A6(#11)(no3)	| G#m |
	| C#m7	| Add9 Badd11	| C#m7	| Add9 Badd11 |
	| C#m7	| Add9 Badd11	| E	| E ||

Verse 1
          C#m7   Bsus4
From the ice-age to the dole-age,
      Amaj7(#11)
There is but one concern,
A6(#11)(no3)   G#m
I have just discovered…

Chorus 1
C#m7   Add9 Badd11
Some girls are bigger than others,
C#m7   Bsus4
Some girls are bigger than others,
Amaj7(#11)   A6(#11)(no3) G#m
   Some girls' mothers are bigger than other girls' mothers.

Chorus 2   As Chorus 1

© Copyright 1986 Marr Songs Limited/Artane Music Incorporated.
Chrysalis Music Limited (50%)/Universal Music Publishing Limited (50%).
All Rights Reserved. International Copyright Secured.

Instrumental | C♯m7 | Add9 Badd11 | C♯m7 | Add9 Badd11 |
            | C♯m7 | Add9 Badd11 | E | E   ‖

Verse 2
    C♯m7   Bsus4
As Anthony said to Cleopatra
    Amaj7(♯11)   A6(♯11)(no3)
As he opened a crate of ale
Emaj7(no5)/G♭   G♯m
Oh,   I   say,

Chorus 3   As Chorus 1

Chorus 4   As Chorus 1

Chorus 5
  C♯m7   Add9   Badd11
     Send me your pillow,
  C♯m7   Bsus4
      The one that you dream on.

| Amaj7(♯11) | A6(♯11)(no3) | Emaj7(no5)/G♯ | G♯m |

  C♯m7   Add9   Badd11
     Send me your pillow,
  C♯m7   Add9   Badd11
      The one that you dream on.
  C♯m7   Add9   Badd11   E
       And I'll send you mine…

Coda   ‖: C♯m7 | Add9 Badd11 | C♯m7 | Add9 Badd11 :‖
Repeat ad lib. to fade

Still ill

Words & Music by
Morrissey & Johnny Marr

Am7   F6   Gsus2   Em7   C   Fsus2   G5

Capo fourth fret

Intro ‖: N.C. | N.C. | N.C. | N.C. :‖

Verse 1

Am7   F6   Gsus2 F6
I decree today that life is simply taking and not giving,
Em7 Am7 F6   Gsus2 F6
England is mine and it owes me a living.
Em7 Am7 F6   Gsus2
Ask me why and I'll spit in your eye,
F6 Em7 Am7   F6 Gsus2 F6
Oh, ask me why and I'll spit in your eye.
Em7   C
But we cannot cling
  Fsus2   G5
To the old dreams anymore,
   Em7 C
No we cannot cling
  Fsus2 G5
To those dreams.
   Am7 F6
Does the body rule the mind
   Gsus2 F6 Em7
Or does the mind rule the body?
  Am7 F6 Gsus2 F6
I dunno…

© Copyright 1984 Marr Songs Limited/Artane Music Incorporated.
Chrysalis Music Limited (50%)/Universal Music Publishing Limited (50%).
All Rights Reserved. International Copyright Secured.

Chorus 1

```
     Em7      Am7 F6      Gsus2 F6
Under the iron bridge we kissed,
        Em7       Am7 F6         Gsus2 F6
And although I ended up with sore lips,
     Em7    C     Fsus2          G5
It just wasn't like the old days anymore.
         Em7   C       Fsus2
No it wasn't like those days,
      G5   C    Fsus2   G5
Am I still ill?
      Em7   C    Fsus2
Oh,
      G5   C    Fsus2   G5
Am I still ill?
      Em7   C    Fsus2   G5
Oh.
```

Verse 2

```
         Am7          F6          Gsus2      F6   Em7
Does the body rule the mind or does the mind rule the body?
       Am7  F6   Gsus2    F6
I dunno.
Em7     Am7        F6      Gsus2
Ask me why and I'll die,
F6  Em7 Am7        F6    Gsus2   F6
Oh,     ask me why and I'll die.
Em7                  C       Fsus2   G5
   And if you must go to work tomorrow,
      Em7        C            Fsus2    G5
Well if I were you I wouldn't bother,
           Am7            F6
For there are brighter sides to life,
              Gsus2         F6       Em7
And I should know because I've seen them,
           Am7   F6   Gsus2   F6
But not often.
```

Chorus 2   As Chorus 1

Coda

| N.C. | N.C. | N.C. | N.C. |
| N.C. | N.C. | N.C. | N.C. Am7 |

Stop Me If You Think You've Heard This One Before

Words & Music by
Morrissey & Johnny Marr

Asus2   G6   C   D   F#
E   Fsus2   Am(add9)   Em7   E7

Capo third fret

Intro | Asus2 | G6 | C | D |
| F# | E | Asus2 | G6 |
| C | D | F# | E ||

Chorus 1
Asus2   G6
Stop me, oh stop me,
C   D
Stop me if you think that you've heard this one before.
Asus2   G6
Stop me, oh stop me,
C   D
Stop me if you think that you've heard this one before.

Verse 1
Asus2   G6
   Nothing's changed,
        C   D
I still love you, oh I still love you,
       Asus2   G6   C   D
Only slightly, only slightly less than I used to, my love.

Instrumental 1 | Fsus2 | Fsus2 | Am(add9) | Am(add9) |
| Fsus2 | Fsus2 | G6 | Em7   G6 ||

© Copyright 1987 Marr Songs Limited/Artane Music Incorporated.
Chrysalis Music Limited (50%)/Universal Music Publishing Limited (50%).
All Rights Reserved. International Copyright Secured.

Verse 2

Asus²   G⁶
I was delayed, I was way-laid,
    C   D
An emergency stop: I smelt the last ten seconds of life.
Asus²   G⁶
    I crashed down on the crossbar,
       C   D   Asus²
And the pain was enough to make a shy, bald buddhist reflect
          G⁶
And plan a mass-murder.
    C   D
Who said I'd lied to her?
    Asus²   G⁶
Oh, who said I'd lied because I never, I never,
C   D
Who said I'd lied, because I never?

Instrumental 2 | Fsus² | Fsus² | Am(add9) | Am(add9) |

                 | Fsus² | Fsus² | G⁶ | Em⁷   G⁶ ||

Verse 3

Asus²   G⁶
I was detained, I was restrained,
          C
And broke my spleen and broke my knee,
      D
(And then he really lays into me.)
Asus²   G⁶
Friday night in outpatients
    C   D
Who said I'd lied to her?
    Asus²   G⁶
Oh, who said I'd lied because I never, I never,
C   D
Who said I'd lied because I never?
    Asus²   G⁶
And so I drank one, it became four,
       C   D
And when I fell on the floor I drank more.

Instrumental 3	Fsus2		Fsus2		Am(add9)		Am(add9)	
	Fsus2		Fsus2		G6		Em7	G6

Chorus 2   As Chorus 1

Verse 4   As Verse 1

Instrumental 4	Asus2		Em7		C		D	
	Asus2		Em7		C		D	
	Asus2		Em7		C		D	
	F♯		E		E7 (fermata)			

Stretch Out And Wait

Words & Music by
Morrissey & Johnny Marr

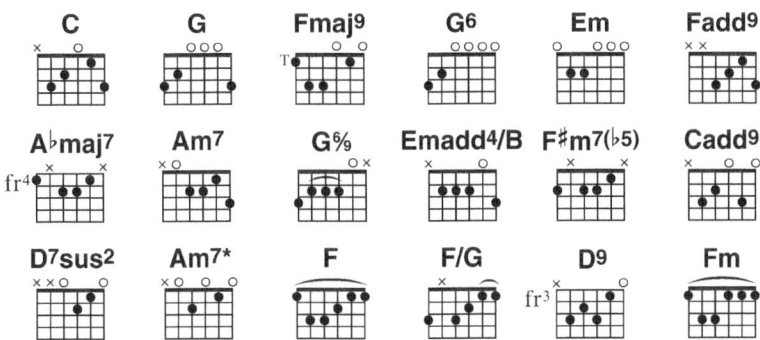

Capo fouth fret

Verse 1
```
        C  G     Fmaj9    G6
         On the high-rise estate,
    Em       C          Fadd9   G6
    What's at the back of your mind?
           C       G      Fmaj9    G6
    Oh the three day debates on a high-rise estate,
    Em       C          Fadd9   G6
    What's at the back of your mind?
```

Verse 2
```
           C      G     Fmaj9      G6
    Two icy-cold hands conducting the way,
         Em     C         Fadd9  G6
    It's the Eskimo blood in my veins.
            C       G      Fmaj9     G6
    Amid concrete and clay and general decay,
    Em        C         Fadd9  G6
    Nature must still find a way.
```

© Copyright 1987 Marr Songs Limited/Artane Music Incorporated.
Chrysalis Music Limited (50%)/Universal Music Publishing Limited (50%).
All Rights Reserved. International Copyright Secured.

Verse 3

   C **G** **Fmaj9** **G6**
So ignore all the codes of the day,
   Em **C**   **Fadd9** **G6**
Let your juvenile impulses sway.
C   **G**   **Fmaj9** **G6**
This way and that way, this way and that way,
Em   **C**   **Fadd9** **G6**
God, how sex implores you,
  A♭maj7
To let yourself lose yourself.

Chorus 1

  Am7   **C**
Stretch out and wait,
  Am7   **G**
Stretch out and wait,
  Am7 **C**   **Fadd9** **G6**
  Let your puny body lie down, lie down.
Fadd9   **G⁶⁄₉**
As we lie, you say,
   Emadd4/B F♯m7(♭5)
As we lie, you say,
Cadd9 **D7sus2**
   Stretch out and
  Am7   **C**
Stretch out and wait.
  Am7   **G**
Stretch out and wait,
  Am7 **C**   **Fadd9** **G6**
  Let your puny body lie down, lie down.
Fadd9   **G⁶⁄₉**
As we lie, you say,
    Am7*   **D7sus2**
"Will the world end in the night time?"
   Fadd9 **G⁶⁄₉**
(I really don't know.)

Chorus 1 (cont.)

     Am7*   D7sus2
"Will the world end in the day time?"
   Fadd9 G%
(I really don't know.)
     Am7*   D7sus2
"And is there any point ever having children?"
   Fadd9 G%
(Oh I don't know.)
  D7sus2   F   F/G
All I do know is we're here and it's now…

Verse 4

   C   G
So stretch out and wait
F   G
Stretch out and wait,
    Em C   Fadd9 G6
There is no debate, no debate, no debate,
C   G   Fmaj9 G6
How can you consciously contemplate,
     Em   C   Fadd9 G6
When there's no debate, no debate?
    C   G
Stretch out and wait,
Fmaj9 G6   Em C Fadd9
  Stretch out and wait,
G6   C   G
Stretch out and wait,_____
Fmaj9 G6 C   G Fmaj9 G6
Wait,_____ wait,_____ wait,_____
C   G Fmaj9 G6
Wait.

| Am7* | D9 | Fm | ‖ |

Suffer Little Children

Words & Music by
Morrissey & Johnny Marr

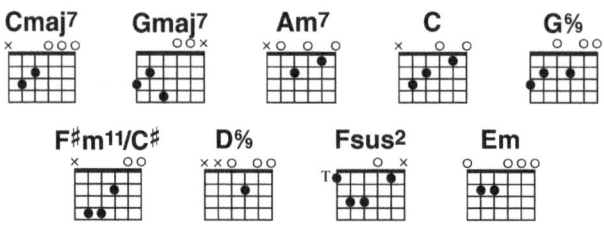

Capo second fret

Intro | Cmaj7 Gmaj7 | Cmaj7 Gmaj7 | Cmaj7 Gmaj7 | Am7 C G% ||

Verse 1
    Cmaj7   Gmaj7 Cmaj7   Gmaj7
Over the moor,   take me to the moor.
    Cmaj7   Gmaj7
Dig a shallow grave,
    Am7   C   G%
And I'll lay me down.
    Cmaj7   Gmaj7 Cmaj7   Gmaj7
Over the moor,   take me to the moor.
    Cmaj7   Gmaj7
Dig a shallow grave,
    Am7   C   G%
And I'll lay me down.
    Am7   D%   F#m11/C#   Fsus2
Lesley-Anne, and your pretty white beads
     G   Em
Oh John, you'll never be a man,
    C   D%   C D% F#m11/C#   Fsus2
And you'll never see your   home again.
    G   Em
    Oh, Manchester,
    C   D%
So much to answer for.

© Copyright 1984 Marr Songs Limited/Artane Music Incorporated.
Chrysalis Music Limited (50%)/Universal Music Publishing Limited (50%).
All Rights Reserved. International Copyright Secured.

Verse 2

  Cmaj7 Gmaj7 Cmaj7 Gmaj7
Edward, see those alluring lights?
  Cmaj7   Gmaj7 Am7 C G%
Tonight will be your very last night.
  Cmaj7   Gmaj7   Cmaj7 Gmaj7
 A woman said, "I know my son is dead,
  Cmaj7   Gmaj7   Am7 C G%
  I'll never rest my hands on his sacred head."
  Am7   D%   F#m11/C# Fsus2
Hindley wakes and Hindley says,
  G   Em C   D%
Hindley wakes, Hindley wakes,
  C   D%   F#m11/C# Fsus2
Hindley wakes and says,
  G   Em   C   D%
"Oh, wherever he has gone, I have gone."

Verse 3

  Cmaj7 Gmaj7 Cmaj7 Gmaj7
But fresh lilaced moorland fields
  Cmaj7 Gmaj7 Am7 C   G%
Cannot hide the stolid stench of death.
  Cmaj7 Gmaj7 Cmaj7   Gmaj7
  Fresh lilaced moorland fields
  Cmaj7 Gmaj7 Am7 C   G%
Cannot hide the stolid stench of death.
  Am7   D%   F#m11/C# Fsus2
Hindley wakes and says,
  G   Em C   D%
Hindley wakes, Hindley wakes,
  C   D%   F#m11/C# Fsus2
Hindley wakes and says,
  G   Em   C   D%
"Oh, whatever he has done, I have done."

Verse 4

    Cmaj7 Gmaj7   Cmaj7   Gmaj7
But this is no easy ride,
Cmaj7 Gmaj7   Am7   C   G%
  For a child   cries:
     Cmaj7 Gmaj7   Cmaj7   Gmaj7
"Oh, find me…   find me, nothing more,
Cmaj7 Gmaj7 Am7   C   G%
We are on a   sullen misty moor,
Am7   D%   F#m11/C# Fsus2
We may be dead and we may be gone,
    G   Em   C   D%
But we will be, we will be,
C   D%   F#m11/C#   Fsus2
We will be right   by your side
G   Em   C   D%
  Until the day you die,   this is no easy ride.

Verse 5

Cmaj7 Gmaj7   Cmaj7   Gmaj7
We will haunt you when you laugh,
Am7 C   G%   Cmaj7   Gmaj7
Yes,   you could say we're a team,
Cmaj7   Gmaj7   Cmaj7   Gmaj7
You might sleep,   you might sleep,
Am7 C   G%   Am7   D%   F#m11/C#   Fsus2
You might sleep, oh…
G   Em   C   D%
  You will never dream!
    C   D%   F#m11/C#   Fsus2
Oh, you might sleep, but you will never dream!
G   Em   C   D%
You might sleep, but you will   never dream!"

Verse 6

     Cmaj7 Gmaj7
       Oh, Manchester,
Cmaj7   Gmaj7   Cmaj7 Gmaj7 Am7 C G%
    So much to answer for.
Cmaj7 Gmaj7
Oh, Manchester,
Cmaj7   Gmaj7   Cmaj7 Gmaj7 Am7 C G%
    So much to answer for.
Am7   D%   F#m11/C# Fsus2
Find me, find me,_____
G   Em
Find me,
C   D%   Am7 D%   F#m11/C# Fsus2
  I'll haunt you when you laugh,
G   Em   C   D%
  I'll haunt you when you laugh.
     Am7   D%   F#m11/C# Fsus2
You might sleep, but you,_____
G   Em   C   D%
  You will never dream.

| Am7 D% | F#m11/C# Fsus2 |

G   Em   C   D%   Am7 D% F#m11/C# Fsus2
Oh, over the moor,   I'm on the moor,
G   Em   C   D%
Oh, over the moor.
    Am7 D% F#m11/C# Fsus2 G   Em C D%   Am7 D%
The child is   on   the   moor.

Coda

‖: F#m11/C# Fsus2 | G   Em | C   D% | Am7 D% :‖
                                                                               Repeat to fade

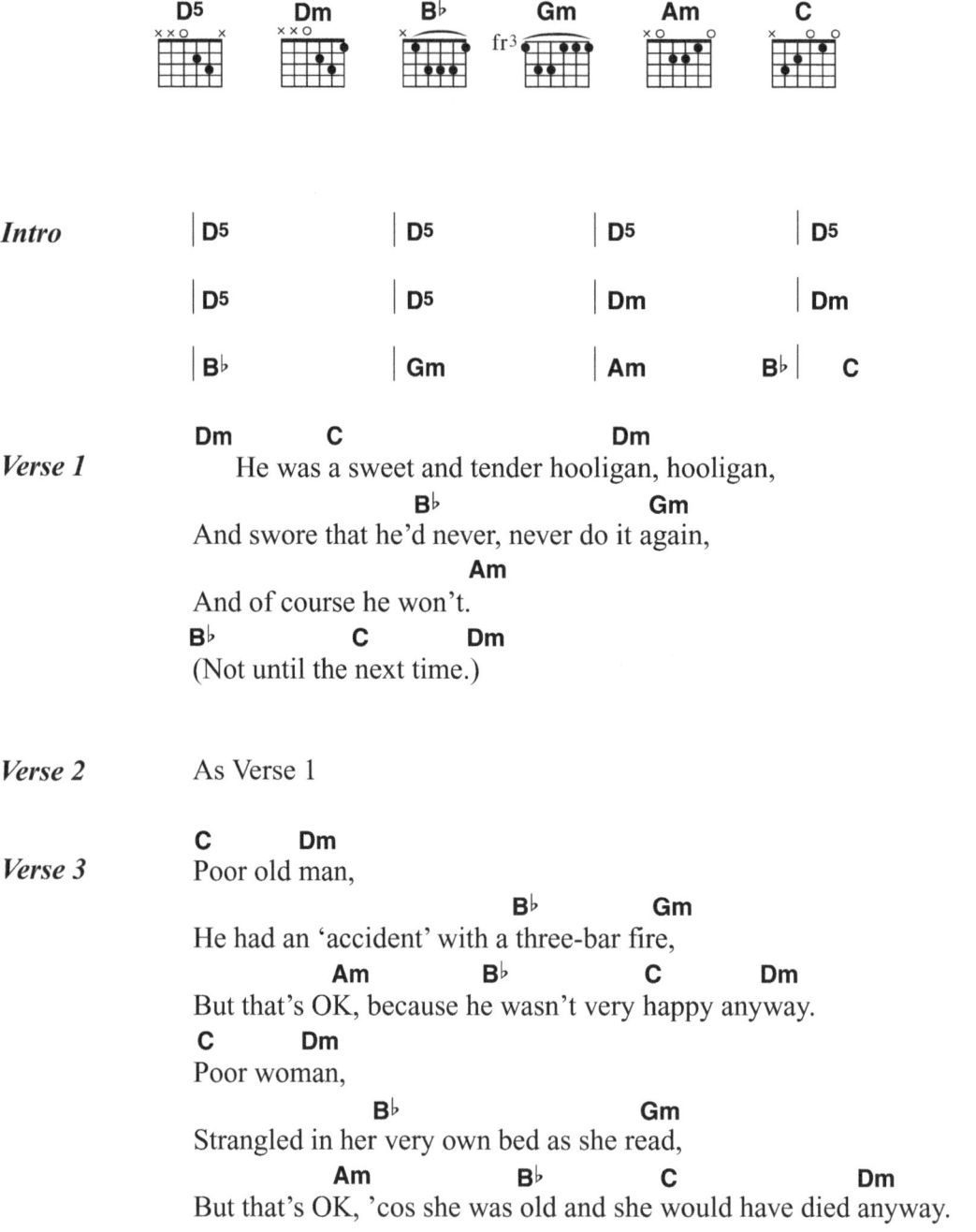

Chorus 1

    C   Dm
  Don't blame this sweet and tender hooligan, hooligan,
     B♭   Gm   Am
  Because he'll never, never, never, never, never, never do it again.
  B♭   C Dm
  (Not until the next time.)

Verse 4

    C   Dm
   Jury you've heard every word but before you decide
  B♭   Gm
  Would you look into those 'mother me' eyes,
      Am
  I love you for you my love, you my love,
  B♭   C   Dm
  You my love, you my love.
    C   Dm
   Jury you've heard every word but before you decide
  B♭   Gm
  Would you look into those 'mother me' eyes,
      Am
  I love you for you my love, you my love,
  B♭   C   Dm
  Love you just for you my love.

Chorus 2

    C   Dm
  Don't blame this sweet and tender hooligan, hooligan,
     B♭   Gm
  Because he'll never, never do it again,
       Am   B♭ C Dm
  And in the midst of life we are in debt, et cetera!
    C   Dm
  Don't blame this sweet and tender hooligan, hooligan,
     B♭   Gm
  Because he'll never, never do it again,
       Am   B♭ C Dm
  And in the midst of life we are in death, et cetera!

Coda

     Dm   B♭   Gm
Et cetera, et cetera, et cetera, et cetera!
       Am   B♭   C   Dm   C
In the midst of life we are in death, et cetera!
     Dm   B♭   Gm
Et cetera, et cetera, et cetera, et cetera!
       Am   B♭   C   Dm   C
In the midst of life we are in death, et cetera!

‖: Dm | Dm | B♭ | Gm |

| Am | B♭ | C | Dm | Dm C :‖

Repeat ad lib.

| Dm | Dm C | Dm | Dm C |

| Dm𝄐 ‖

That Joke Isn't Funny Anymore

Words & Music by
Morrissey & Johnny Marr

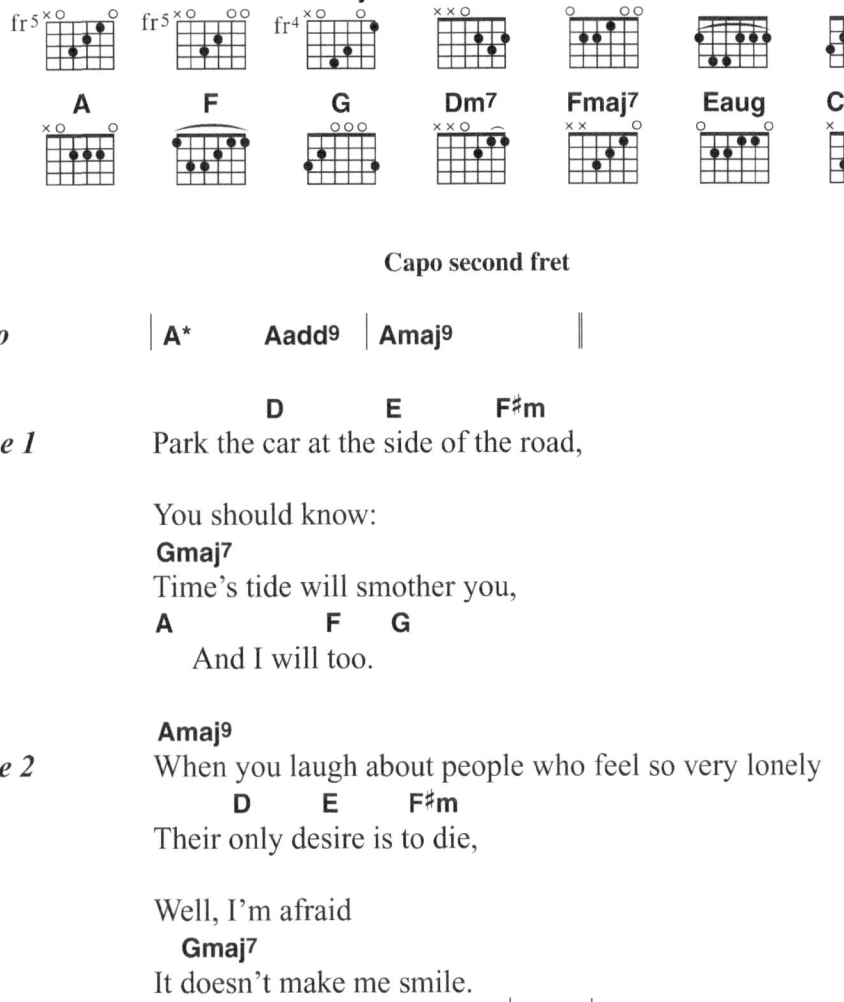

Capo second fret

Intro | A*   Aadd9 | Amaj9 ||

Verse 1
        D   E   F#m
Park the car at the side of the road,

You should know:
Gmaj7
Time's tide will smother you,
A   **F**   **G**
  And I will too.

Verse 2
       Amaj9
When you laugh about people who feel so very lonely
      D   E   F#m
Their only desire is to die,

Well, I'm afraid
  Gmaj7
It doesn't make me smile.
A   **F**   **G** |**F** |**D**
  I wish I could laugh.

© Copyright 1985 Marr Songs Limited/Artane Music Incorporated.
Chrysalis Music Limited (50%)/Universal Music Publishing Limited (50%).
All Rights Reserved. International Copyright Secured.

Chorus 1

        F   G   C   D
But that joke isn't funny anymore.
   F
It's too close to home
       Dm7
And it's too near the bone.
     Fmaj7
It's too close to home
     C
And it's too near the bone.
         Fmaj7 | A | Fmaj7 G |
More than you'll ever know.

Bridge

   A   Eaug Gmaj7
         Kick them when they fall down,
Cmaj7   D
  Kick them when they fall down.
   A   Eaug Gmaj7
         Kick them when they fall down,
Cmaj7   D
  Kick them when they fall down.
   A   Eaug Gmaj7
         Kick them when they fall down,
Cmaj7   D
  Kick them when they fall down.
   A   Eaug Gmaj7
         You kick them when they fall down,
Cmaj7   D | F | D
  Kick them when they fall down.

Verse 3

        F   G   C   D
It was dark as I drove the point home,
   F
And on cold leather seats,
     Dm7
Well, it suddenly struck me:
Fmaj7   C   Fmaj7
   I just might die with a smile on my face after all.

  | A | Fmaj7 G | A | Eaug | Gmaj7 ||

Coda

    Cmaj7 D   **A**   **Eaug**
I've seen this happen in other people's lives,
    Gmaj7   **Cmaj7**
And now it's happening in mine.
D   **A**   **Eaug**
I've seen this happen in other people's lives,
    Gmaj7   **Cmaj7**
And now it's happening in mine.
D   **A**   **Eaug**
I've seen this happen in other people's lives,
    Gmaj7   **Cmaj7**
And now it's happening in mine.
D   **A**   **Eaug**
I've seen this happen in other people's lives,
    Gmaj7   **Cmaj7**
And now it's happening in mine.
D   **A**   **Eaug**
I've seen this happen in other people's lives,
    Gmaj7 **Cmaj7** **D**   **A**
And now,   now it's happening in mine.
       Eaug
Happening in mine,
      Gmaj7
Happening in mine,
      Cmaj7
Happening in mine,
D
I've seen this happen…

‖: **A** | **Eaug** | **Gmaj7** | **Cmaj7 D**   :‖
Repeat w/vocal ad lib. to fade

There Is A Light That Never Goes Out

Words by Morrissey
Music by Johnny Marr

Am   F   G   C   Dm

Capo fourth fret

Intro

| Am | F G ||

Verse 1

    Am   G   Am G   F   C G
Take me out   tonight
                Am   G
Where there's music and there's people
            Am   G   F   C G
Who are young and alive. ___
Am G   Am G
Driving in your car
 F   C
I never, never want to go home
        G   Am   G Am G   F   C G
Because I haven't got one   anymore.

Verse 2

    Am   G   Am G   F   C G
Take me out   tonight
               Am   G   Am   C   F C G
Because I want to see people and I want to see lights. ___
Am G   Am G
Driving in your car
 F   C
Oh please don't drop me home
  G   Am   G
Because it's not my home, it's their home
        Am   G   F   C G
And I'm welcome no more.

© Copyright 1986 Bona Relations Limited (50%)/
Marr Songs Limited/Universal Music Publishing Limited (50%).
All Rights Reserved. International Copyright Secured.

Chorus 1

```
        Dm F      G    C          Am  F
           And if a double-decker bus   crashes into us
      G         C             F             Dm
        To die by your side is such a heavenly way to die.
              C       Am  F
    And if a ten-ton truck,   kills the both of us
      G         C             F                    Dm
        To die by your side; well the pleasure, the privilege is mine.
```

Verse 3

```
    Am   G      Am  G   F   C
        Take me out     tonight
    G      Am              G
    Take me anywhere, I don't care,
           Am        G   F  C G
    I don't care, I don't care.
              Am       G   Am    G
    And in the darkened underpass I thought
          F                          C  G
    "Oh God, my chance has come at last," ___
                Am        G
    But then a strange fear gripped me
         Am         G   F  C G
    And I just couldn't ask.
```

Verse 4

```
    Am   G      Am  G   F
        Take me out     tonight,
    C     G       Am               G
       Oh take me anywhere, I don't care,
           Am        G   F  C G
    I don't care, I don't care. _____
    Am    G      Am   G
    Driving in your car
         F                  C
    I never, never want to go home
            G         Am    G            Am
    Because I haven't got one, oh-del dum,
    G          F        C G
    Oh I haven't got one.
```

Chorus 2   As Chorus 1

Coda

```
             Am       G        Am        G
       ||: Oh, there is a light and it never goes out,
       F                  C             G
       There is a light and it never goes out.   :||   Play 4 times

            ||: Am  G  | Am  G  | F       | C   G  :||   Repeat to fade
```

153

This Charming Man

Words & Music by
Morrissey & Johnny Marr

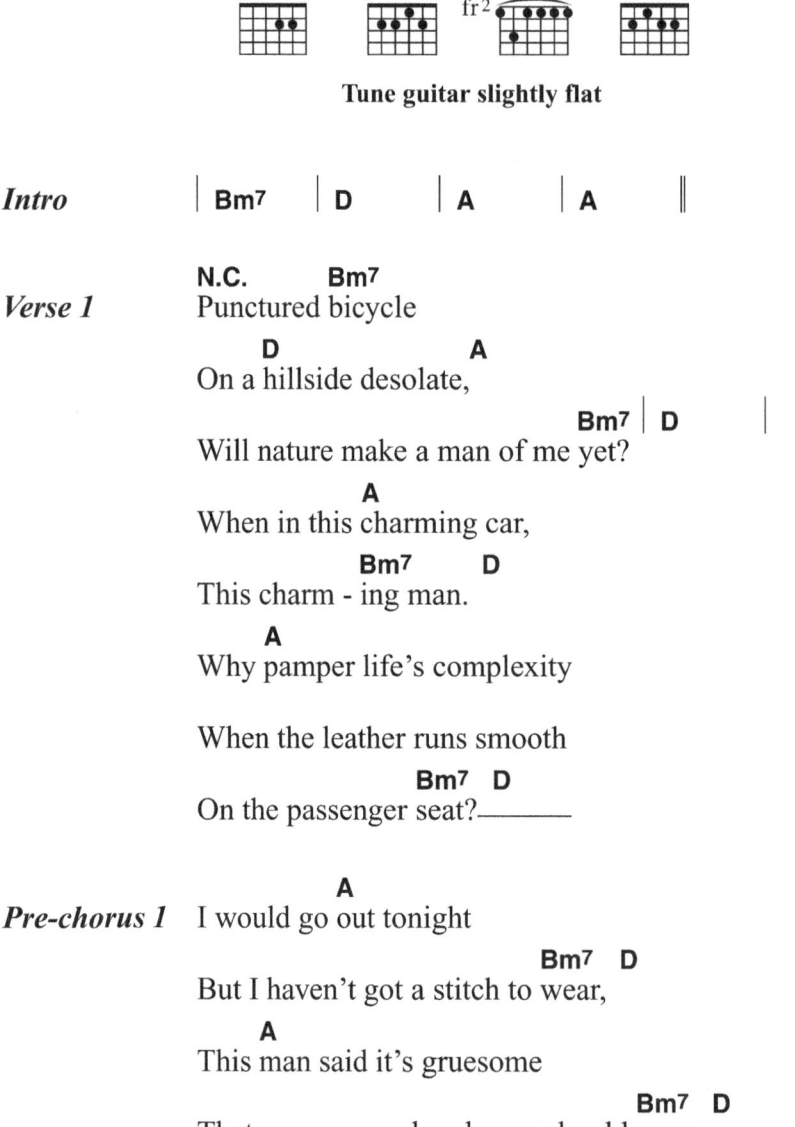

Tune guitar slightly flat

Intro | Bm7 | D | A | A ||

Verse 1

      N.C.   Bm7
Punctured bicycle
     D   A
On a hillside desolate,
                         Bm7 D
Will nature make a man of me yet?
              A
When in this charming car,
        Bm7   D
This charm - ing man.
    A
Why pamper life's complexity

When the leather runs smooth
                 Bm7 D
On the passenger seat?———

Pre-chorus 1

      A
I would go out tonight
                   Bm7 D
But I haven't got a stitch to wear,
    A
This man said it's gruesome
                     Bm7 D
That someone so handsome should care.———

	Dmaj9 E6 F♯m7
Chorus 1	Ah! A jumped-up pantry boy

                B9   Dmaj9
              Who never knew his place,

                B9   F♯m7
              He said, "Re - turn the ring".

                Dmaj9   E6   F♯m7   B9
              He knows so much a - bout these things,

                Dmaj9   E6   F♯m7
              He knows so much a - bout these things.

	N.C. A
Pre-chorus 2	I would go out tonight

                                  Bm7 D
              But I haven't got a stitch to wear,

              A
              This man said it's gruesome

                                    |Bm7 D
              That someone so handsome should care___

              A   Bm7   D
              La, la-la, la-la, la-la, this charm - ing man___

              A   Bm7   D
              Oh, la-la, la-la, la-la, this charm - ing man___

	Dmaj9 E6 F♯m7
Chorus 2	Ah! a jumped-up pantry boy

                B9   Dmaj9
              Who never knew his place,

                B9   F♯m7
              He said, "Re - turn the ring".

                Dmaj9   E6   F♯m7   B9
              He knows so much about these things,

                Dmaj9   E6   F♯m7
              He knows so much a - bout these things.

                Dmaj9   E6   F♯m7 B9   Dmaj9   B9   F♯m7
              He knows so much a - bout   these   things.___

Outro	| Dmaj9 | E6 | F♯m7 | B9 | Dmaj9 | B9 | F♯m7 | F♯m7 ||

This Night Has Opened My Eyes

Words & Music by
Morrissey & Johnny Marr

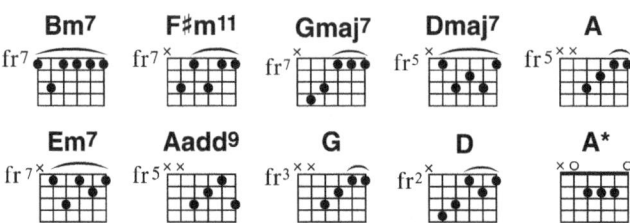

Verse 1

       Bm7   F♯m11   Bm7   F♯m11
In a river the colour of lead,
   Gmaj7   Dmaj7   Gmaj7   A
Immerse the baby's head.
       Bm7   F♯m11
Wrap her up in the News Of The World,
Bm7   F♯m11   Gmaj7   Dmaj7   Gmaj7   A
  Dump her on a doorstep, girl.
      Em7   Bm7
This night has opened my eyes,
     Aadd9
And I will never sleep again.

Verse 2

    Bm7   F♯m11   Bm7   F♯m11
  You kicked and cried like a bullied child,
  Gmaj7   Dmaj7   Gmaj7   A
  A grown man of twenty-five.
      Bm7   F♯m11
Oh, he said he'd cure your ills,
Bm7   F♯m11   Gmaj7 Dmaj7   Gmaj7   A
  But he didn't and he never will.
    Em7   Bm7
Oh,   save your life,
                Aadd9
Because you've only got one.

© Copyright 1984 Marr Songs Limited/Artane Music Incorporated.
Chrysalis Music Limited (50%)/Universal Music Publishing Limited (50%).
All Rights Reserved. International Copyright Secured.

Chorus 1

       Gmaj7   Dmaj7
The dream is gone but the baby is real,
  A   Gmaj7   Em7
  Oh, you did a good thing.
G A   Gmaj7 Dmaj7
  She could have been a poet or she could have been a fool,
  A   Gmaj7   Em7
  Oh, you did a bad thing.
G   A   Em7   G   D A*
  And I'm not happy and I'm not sad.

Verse 3

  Bm7   F#m11   Bm7 F#m11
    A shoeless child on a swing,
  Gmaj7   Dmaj7   Gmaj7
Reminds you of your own again.
  A   Bm7   F#m11
She took away your troubles,
    Bm7   F#m11   Gmaj7 Dmaj7 Gmaj7 A
Oh, but then again she left pain.
  Em7   Bm7
So   please save your life,
              Aadd9
Because you've only got one.

Chorus 2   As Chorus 1

Coda

‖: Gmaj7 Dmaj7 | A   Gmaj7 | Em7 | G   A :‖

      Em7   G   D A*
And I'm not happy and I'm not sad.

‖: Gmaj7 Dmaj7 | A   Gmaj7 | Em7 | G   A :‖

      Em7   G   D A*
And I'm not happy and I'm not sad.

‖: Gmaj7 Dmaj7 | A   Gmaj7 | Em7 | G   A :‖

| Em7 | G   D   A* ‖ *To fade*

These Things Take Time

Words & Music by
Morrissey & Johnny Marr

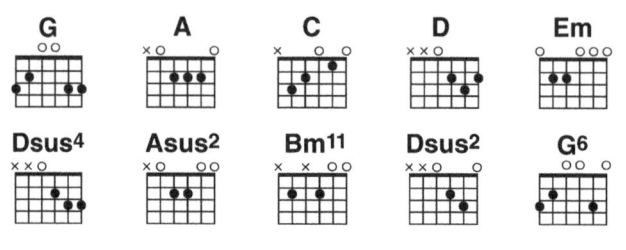

Capo second fret

Intro | G   A | G   A | C   D | C   D ||

Verse 1
       Em   Dsus4   Asus2   Bm11   Dsus2
Mine eyes have seen the glory of the sacred Wunderkind,
      Em   Dsus4   Asus2   Bm11   Dsus2
You took me behind a disused railway line
             Em   Dsus4
And said, "I know a place where we can go,
Asus2   Bm11 Dsus2
 Where we are not known,"
      Em
And you gave me something
      Dsus4   Asus2   Bm11 Dsus2
That I won't forget too soon.

Chorus 1
       G   A   G   A
But I can't believe that you'd ever care,
   C   D   C   D
And this is why you will never care:
Em   Asus2
  For these things take time,
G6   Asus2
 I know that I'm
    Em   Asus2
The most inept that ever stepped.

| G | G | G   C   Dsus2 | Dsus2 ||

Verse 2

```
     Em     Dsus4     Asus2            Bm11  Dsus2
        I'm spellbound, oh but a woman divides,
              Em              Dsus4         Asus2  Bm11 Dsus2
        And the hills are alive with celibate cries.
              Em
        But you know where you came from,
                Dsus4
        You know where you're going.
                Asus2        Bm11   Dsus2
        And you know where you belong,
        Em              Dsus4                 Asus2   Bm11  Dsus2
           You said I was ill, and you were not wrong.
```

Chorus 2

```
             G      A         G     A
        But I can't believe that you'd ever care,
             C      D         C     D
        And so you never care.
        Em                    Asus2
           But these things take time,
        G6            Asus2
           I know that I'm
              Em              Asus2
        The most inept that ever stepped.
```

Bridge

```
        | G            | G             | G     C  Dsus2 | Dsus2          ||
```

Verse 3

```
        Em      Dsus4        Asus2
        Oh, the alcoholic afternoons,
        Bm11         Dsus2     Em
           When we sat in your room,
                   Dsus4         Asus2
        They meant more to me than any,
             Bm11      Dsus2       Em
        Than any living thing on earth.
              Dsus4          Asus2    Bm11  Dsus2   Em
        It had more worth than any     living thing on earth,
            Dsus4    Asus2    Bm11  Dsus2
        On earth, on earth, oh.
```

159

Instrumental | G A | G A | C D | C D ||

Coda
      Em   **Asus²**
      Vivid and in your prime,
      G⁶   **Asus²**
          You will leave me behind,
      Em   **Asus²**
          You will leave me behind.

| G C G | G | G C Dsus² | Dsus² ||

Unloveable

Words & Music by
Morrissey & Johnny Marr

D C G A
F#m7 Gsus2 E7 Bm

Intro

| D C | G A | D C | G A |
| D C | G A | D C | G A ||

Verse 1

   D C G A
  I know I'm unloveable,
   D C   G A
  You don't have to tell me.
       D   C G
  I don't have much in my life,
   A   D C G A
  But take it, it's yours.
       D   C G
  I don't have much in my life,
   A   D C G A
  But take it, it's yours.

Verse 2

   D C G A
  I know I'm unloveable,
   D C   G A
  You don't have to tell me.
F#m7   Gsus2
  Message received loud and clear,
E7   Bm G A
  Loud and clear.
   D   C   G
  I don't have much in my life
   A   D C G A
  But take it, it's yours.

© Copyright 1987 Marr Songs Limited/Artane Music Incorporated.
Chrysalis Music Limited (50%)/Universal Music Publishing Limited (50%).
All Rights Reserved. International Copyright Secured.

Verse 3

```
     D   C          G   A
    I know I'm unloveable,
     D   C          G   A
    You don't have to tell me.
      F#m7            Gsus2
    For  message received loud and clear,
                  E7              Bm  G   A
    Loud and clear, message received.
     D         C         G
    I don't have much in my life
       A           D  C  G   A
    But take it, it's yours.
```

Verse 4

```
            D          C
    I wear black on the outside,
          G         A      D   C  G   A
    'Cos black is how I feel on the inside.
            D          C
    I wear black on the outside,
          G         A      D   C  G   A
    'Cos black is how I feel on the inside.
            D         C
    And if I seem a little strange,
          G          A    D   C  G   A
    Well, that's because I am.
            D         C
    And if I seem a little strange,
          G          A    D   C  G   A
    Well, that's because I am.
       F#m7                 Gsus2
    But I  know that you would like me,

    If only you could see me,
    E7                    Bm  G   A
       If only you could meet me.
```

Verse 4
(cont.)

       D   C   G
I don't have much in my life,
 A   D C G   A
But take it, it's yours.
             D   C
I don't have much in my life,
G   A   D C   G   A
But take it, it's yours.

Instrumental | F♯m7 | Gsus2 | E7 |

‖: Bm   G   A | Bm   F♯m7 G | Bm   G   A | Bm   F♯m7 G :‖
                                                                Repeat to fade

Unhappy Birthday

Words & Music by
Morrissey & Johnny Marr

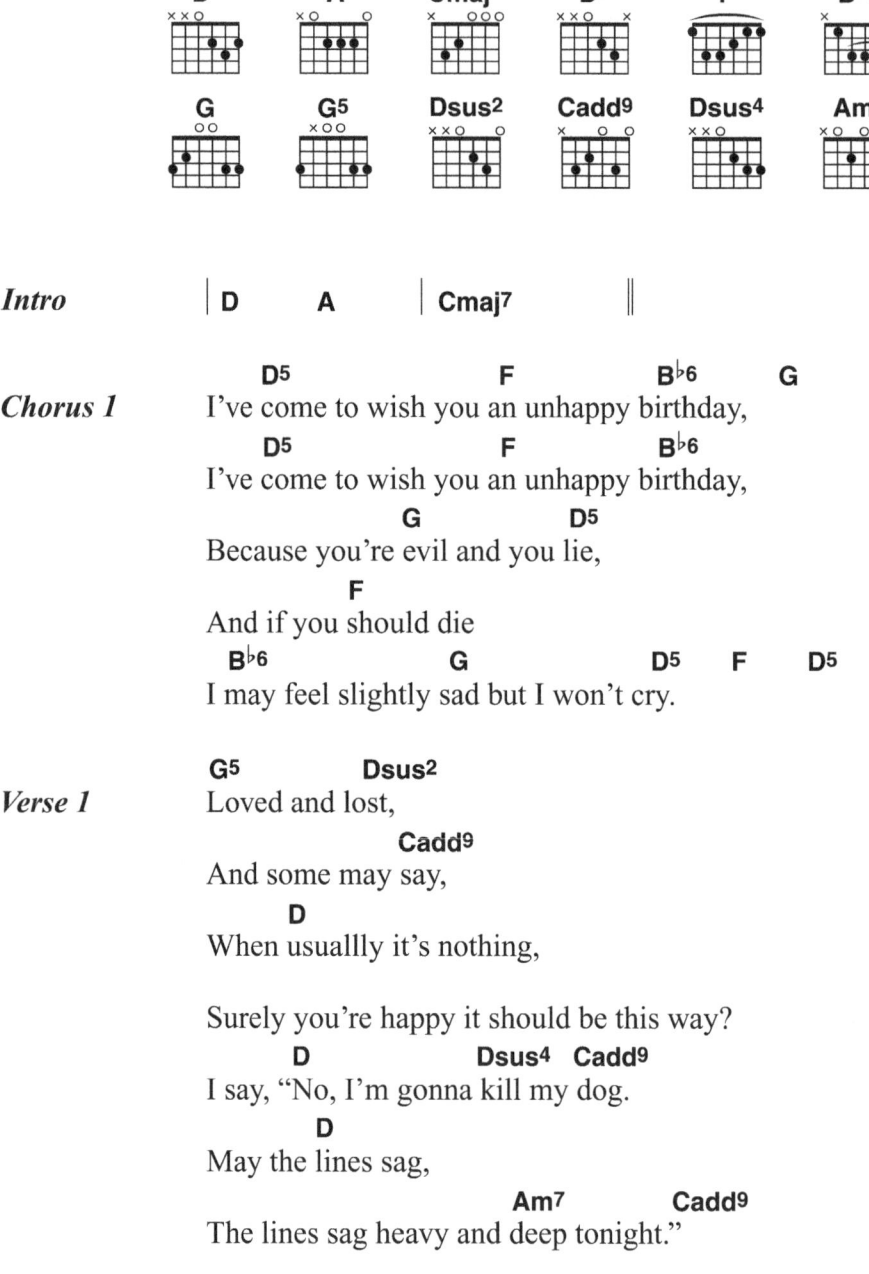

Intro | D   A | Cmaj7 ||

Chorus 1
      D5   F   B♭6   G
I've come to wish you an unhappy birthday,
      D5   F   B♭6
I've come to wish you an unhappy birthday,
               G   D5
Because you're evil and you lie,
        F
And if you should die
 B♭6   G   D5   F   D5
I may feel slightly sad but I won't cry.

Verse 1
    G5   Dsus2
Loved and lost,
             Cadd9
And some may say,
     D
When usuallly it's nothing,

Surely you're happy it should be this way?
        D   Dsus4 Cadd9
I say, "No, I'm gonna kill my dog.
    D
May the lines sag,
                 Am7   Cadd9
The lines sag heavy and deep tonight."

© Copyright 1987 Marr Songs Limited/Artane Music Incorporated.
Chrysalis Music Limited (50%)/Universal Music Publishing Limited (50%).
All Rights Reserved. International Copyright Secured.

Chorus 2   As Chorus 1

Verse 2

     G5   **Dsus2**
Loved and lost,
                   Cadd9
And some may say,
    D
When usuallly it's nothing,
                       Am7   **Cadd9**
Surely you're happy it should be this way?
       D   **Dsus4** **Cadd9**
I said, "No," and then I shot myself,
     D   **Am7** **Cadd9**
So, drink, drink, drink and be ill tonight.

Coda

       D5   **F**   **B♭6**
From_____ the one you left behind,
     G   **D5**
From the one you left behind.
     F   **B♭6**
From the one you left behind,
     G   **(D5)**
From the one you left behind.

‖: **D5** | **F** | **B♭6** | **G**   :‖

*Repeat w/vocal
ad lib. to fade*

Vicar In A Tutu

Words & Music by
Morrissey & Johnny Marr

E   E7   C#m   A   B

Verse 1

      E   E7
I was minding my business,
  E   E7
Lifting some lead off
      E   E7   E   E7
The roof of the Holy Name church.
          E   E7   E   E7
It was worthwhile living a laughable life,
  E   E7   E   E7
To set my eyes on a blistering sight
          C#m
Of a vicar in a tutu.

He's not strange,
      A   B
He just wants to live his life this way.

Verse 2

        E   E7
A scanty bit of a thing
    E   E7
With a decorative ring,
          E   E7   E   E7
That wouldn't cover the head of a goose.
  E   E7   E   E7
As Rose collects the money in the canister
E   E7   E   E7
Who comes sliding down the banister?
       C#m
The vicar in a tutu.

He's not strange,
      A   B
He just wants to live his life this way.

© Copyright 1986 Marr Songs Limited/Artane Music Incorporated.
Chrysalis Music Limited (50%)/Universal Music Publishing Limited (50%).
All Rights Reserved. International Copyright Secured.

Verse 3

       E   E7
The monkish monsignor
     E   E7
With a head full of plaster
      E   E7   E   E7
Said, "My man, get your vile soul dry-cleaned"
       E   E7   E   E7
As Rose counts the money in the canister,
     E   E7   E
As natural as rain he dances again.
      E7   C♯m   A   B
My God, vicar in a tutu, oh yeah, oh yeah, yeah, yeah, yeah, yeah.

Instrumental | E   E7 | E   E7 | E   E7 | E   E7 |

                  | E   E7 | E   E7 | E   E7 | E   E7 ||

          C♯m   A   B
Vicar in a tutu, oh yeah.

Verse 4

        E   E7
The next day in the pulpit
    E   E7
With freedom and ease,
        E   E7   E   E7
Combating ignorance, dust and disease.
      E   E7   E   E7
As Rose counts the money in the canister,
     E   E7   E   E7
As natural as rain he dances again and again and again.
              C♯m
In the fabric of a tutu

Any man could get used to,
  A   B   C♯m
And I am the living sign, I'm a living sign,
  A   B   C♯m
I am a living sign, I'm a living sign,
  A   B   C♯m
I am a living sign, I'm a living sign,
  A   B
I am a living sign.

Well I Wonder

Words & Music by
Morrissey & Johnny Marr

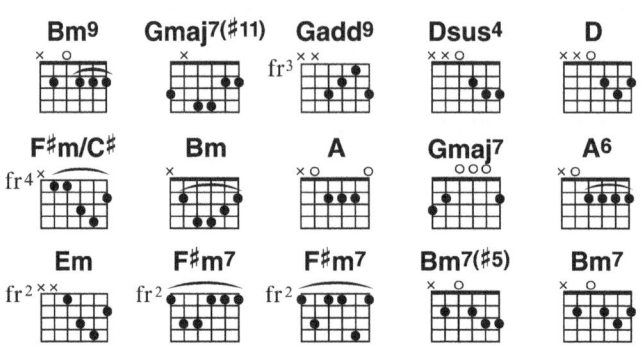

Intro	| Bm9	| Bm9	| Gmaj7(#11)	| Gmaj7(#11)	|
	| Bm9	| Bm9	| Gadd9	| Gadd9	|
	| Bm A	| Bm	| Gadd9	| Gadd9	||

Verse 1
    Dsus4   D   Dsus4   D   F#m/C#
                        Well I won - der,
      Bm   A
Do you hear me when you sleep?
Bm   Gmaj7   A6
 I   hoarsely cry.

Verse 2
    Dsus4   D   Dsus4   D   F#m/C#
                        Well I won - der,
      Bm   A
Do you see me when we pass?
Bm   Gmaj7   A6
 I   half   die.

Chorus 1
Em   Gmaj7   A6
  Please keep me in mind,
Em   Gmaj7   A6
  Please keep me in mind.

Instrumental 1	| Bm9	| Bm9	| Gadd9	| Gadd9	||

© Copyright 1985 Marr Songs Limited/Artane Music Incorporated.
Chrysalis Music Limited (50%)/Universal Music Publishing Limited (50%).
All Rights Reserved. International Copyright Secured.

Bridge

    Dsus⁴ D   F♯m   Bm   Gmaj7
                Gasping, but somehow still alive,
        Em   Gmaj7 A6
This is the fierce last stand of all I am.
Gmaj7 A6 Dsus⁴ D F♯m Bm
Gasp - ing, dying,   but somehow still alive,
        Em   Gmaj7 A6
This is the   final stand of all   I am.

Chorus 2

Gmaj7 A6 Em   Gmaj7   A6   Gmaj7 A6
Please   keep me in mind.

Instrumental *(w/vocal ad lib.)*

Bm9	Bm9	Gmaj7(♯11)	Gmaj7(♯11)
Bm A	Bm	Gadd9	Gadd9
Dsus⁴ D	F♯m F♯m7	Bm7(♯5) Bm7	Gmaj7 A6
Em7	Em7	Gmaj7	A6 Gmaj7 A6
Dsus⁴ D	F♯m F♯m7	Bm7(♯5) Bm7	Gmaj7 A6
Em7	Em7	Gmaj7	A6 Gmaj7 A6
Em7	Em7	Gmaj7	A6 Gmaj7 A6
Em7	Em7	Gmaj7	A6 Gmaj7 A6
Bm9	Bm9	Gmaj7(♯11)	Gmaj7(♯11)
Bm9	Bm9	Gadd9	Gadd9
Bm A	Bm	Gadd9	Gadd9
|: Bm A	Bm	Gmaj7	A6 Gmaj7 A6 :|

Play 3 times

| Bm A | Bm | Gadd9 | ||

What Difference Does It Make?

Words & Music by
Morrissey & Johnny Marr

A5   D5   E   F#m   Dsus2

Capo second fret

Intro

‖: A riff |
| A open (5) | A 2fr (3) | E 2fr (4) | G open (3) | A 2fr (3) | A 2fr (3) | E 2fr (4) | G open (3) |

| C riff | | | | D riff | | | |
| C 3fr (5) | A 2fr (3) | E 2fr (4) | G open (3) | A 2fr (3) | D 3fr (2) | E 2fr (4) | G open (3) | :‖

Verse 1

    A riff   C riff   D riff   A riff
All men have secrets and here is mine, so let it be known.
            C riff
We have been through hell and high tide,
  D riff   A riff
I can surely rely on you.
      C riff
And yet you start to recoil,
  D riff   A riff
Heavy words are so lightly thrown,
      C riff   D riff
But still I'd leap in front of a flying bullet for you.

Chorus 1

  A5   D5   E   D5
So what difference does it make?
  A5   D5   E   D5
So what difference does it make?
F#m   Dsus2   F#m   Dsus2
It makes none, but, now   you have gone,
  F#m   Dsus2   A riff
And you must be looking very old tonight.

© Copyright 1984 Marr Songs Limited/Artane Music Incorporated.
Chrysalis Music Limited (50%)/Universal Music Publishing Limited (50%).
All Rights Reserved. International Copyright Secured.

Verse 2

    (A riff)   C riff   D riff   A riff
The devil will find work for idle hands to do,
           C riff   D riff   A riff
I stole and I lied, and why? Because you asked me to.
                C riff
But now you make me feel so ashamed,
          D riff   A riff
Because I've only got two hands,
             C riff   D riff
Well, I'm still fond of you, oh.

Chorus 2

    A5   D5   E   D5
    So what difference does it make?
    A5   D5   E   D5
    So what difference does it make?
F♯m   Dsus2   F♯m   Dsus2
Oh, It makes none, but,   now you have gone,
    F♯m   Dsus2   A riff
And your prejudice won't keep you warm tonight.

Verse 3

    (A riff)   C riff   D riff   A riff
Oh the devil will find work for idle hands to do,
           C riff   D riff   A riff
I stole and then I lied just because you asked me to.
                C riff
But now you know the truth about me,
         D riff   A riff
You won't see me anymore,
             C riff   D riff
Well, I'm still fond of you, oh.

Chorus 3

  A5   D5   E   D5
    But no more apologies,
  A5   D5   E   D5
    No more apologies.
F♯m   Dsus2 F♯m   Dsus2
Oh, I'm too tired,   I'm so very tired,
    F♯m   Dsus2   A riff
And I'm feeling very sick and ill today,
             C riff   D riff
But I'm still fond of you, oh.

Coda

‖: A riff | C riff | D riff   :‖
Repeat ad lib. to fade

What She Said

Words & Music by
Morrissey & Johnny Marr

Chords: F#5, E5, B5, D5, C#5, A5, E5*

Intro

| F#5 | E5 | B5 | D5 C#5 |
| A5 | B5 | D5 | E5* |

Verse 1

     F#5
What she said:
    E5   B5   D5 C#5
"How come someone hasn't noticed that I'm dead
     A5   B5
And decided to bury me? God knows, I'm ready!"
D5   E5*
La-la-la-la-la.

Verse 2

     F#5   E5
What she said was sad,
      B5   D5 C#5
But then, all the rejection she's had,
    A5
To pretend to be happy
    B5
Could only be idiocy.
D5   E5*
La-la-la-li-di-da-da-da.

Verse 3

     F#5   E5   B5
What she said was not for the job or
   D5   C#5
Lover that she never had.
| A5 | B5 | D5 | E5* |
Oh,

No, no, no.

© Copyright 1985 Marr Songs Limited/Artane Music Incorporated.
Chrysalis Music Limited (50%)/Universal Music Publishing Limited (50%).
All Rights Reserved. International Copyright Secured.

	F♯5		A5	E5		F♯5			A5	E5	
Instrumental 1											
	F♯5		A5	E5		A5	B5		D5	E5*	‖

Verse 4

       F♯5   E5
What she read, all heady books,
    B5   D5   C♯5
She'd sit and prophesise.
      A5   B5
It took a tattooed boy from Birkenhead
 D5   E5*
To really, really open her eyes.

Verse 5

As Verse 4

Verse 6

     F♯5
What she said:
  E5   B5   D5   C♯5
"I smoke 'cos I'm hoping for an early death,
  A5 B5   D5   E5*
And I need to cling to something!"

Verse 7

     F♯5
What she said:
  E5   B5   D5   C♯5
"I smoke 'cos I'm hoping for an early death,
  A5 B5   D5   E5*
And I need to cling to something!"

No, no, no, no.

	F♯5		A5	E5		F♯5			A5	E5	
Instrumental 2											
	F♯5		A5	E5		A5	B5		D5	E5*	
	‖: F♯5		E5			B5			D5	C♯5	
	A5		B5			D5			E5*		:‖
										Play 3 times	
	F♯5		E5			B5			D5	C♯5	‖

William, It Was Really Nothing

Words & Music by
Morrissey & Johnny Marr

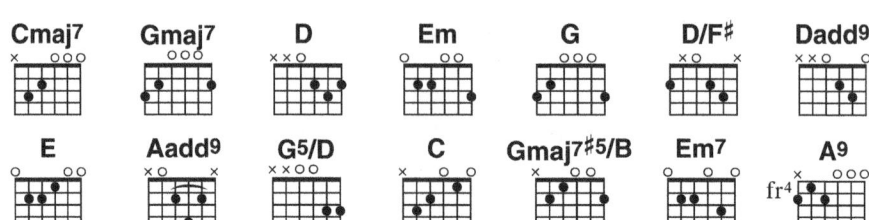

Capo seventh fret

Intro | Cmaj7 | Gmaj7 | D | Em ||

Verse 1
    Cmaj7   Gmaj7   D   Em
The rain falls hard on a humdrum town,
Cmaj7   Gmaj7   D   Em
  This town has dragged you down.
        Cmaj7   Gmaj7   D   Em
Oh, the rain falls hard on a humdrum town,
Cmaj7
  This town has dragged you down.
G   D/F#   Cmaj7   Dadd9
      And everybody's got to live their life,
    E
And God knows I've got to live mine,
    Gmaj7   Aadd9   E   Eadd9
God knows I've got to live mine.

Instrumental | Gmaj7 | Aadd9 | F | C |
| G5/D | D   C D ||

Chorus 1
    C   G   C   D   Em   Gmaj7#5/B
Willi - am, William it was really nothing,
    C   G   C   D   Em   Gmaj7#5/B
Willi - am, William it was really nothing,
  Em7   A9
    It was your life.

© Copyright 1984 Marr Songs Limited/Artane Music Incorporated.
Chrysalis Music Limited (50%)/Universal Music Publishing Limited (50%).
All Rights Reserved. International Copyright Secured.

Bridge

```
         F   C                    G5/D         D              C   D
         How can you stay    with a fat girl  who'll say:
                    C                G
         "Would you like to marry me?
                    C                     D
         And if you like you can buy the ring."
         Em                  B(♭6)
         She doesn't care about anything.
                    C                G
         Would you like to marry me?
                    C                     D
         And if you like you can buy the ring,
         Em                  B(♭6)      Em7        A9
         I don't dream about anyone   except my - self."
```

Instrumental | Gmaj7 | Aadd9 | F | C |

| G5/D | D   C   D ‖

Chorus 2

```
            C    G   C       D      Em   B(♭6)
         Oh, Willi - am, William it was   really nothing,
            C    G   C       D
         Willi - am, William.
```

Coda | Em | B(♭6) | Em7 | A9   ‖

Wonderful Woman

Words & Music by
Morrissey & Johnny Marr

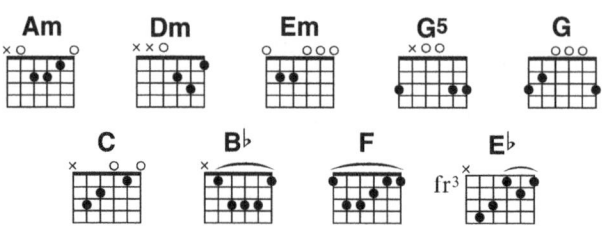

Verse 1

    Am   Dm   Em
Here, her head she lay,
Am   G5   Am   G
Until she'd rise and say:
     Am   Dm   Em
"I'm starved of mirth;
Am   G5   Am   G
Let's go and trip a dwarf."
   Em   C   Am G5 Am G
Oh,   what to be done with her?
   Em   C   B♭   C
Oh,   what to be done with her?

| Am Dm | F   G | F | F |
Oh...
| Am Dm | F   G | F | F ||
Oh...

© Copyright 1992 Marr Songs Limited/Artane Music Incorporated.
Chrysalis Music Limited (50%)/Universal Music Publishing Limited (50%).
All Rights Reserved. International Copyright Secured.

Verse 2

```
         Am   Dm   Em
         Ice  water for blood,
         Am            G5        Am     G
            With neither heart or spine.
                  Am    Dm       Em
         And then just to pass time,
         Am            G5        Am   G
         Let us go and rob the blind.
         Em           C              Am   G5
            What to be done with her?
         Am   G
            I ask myself,
         Em           C           B♭    C
            What to be said of her ?
        | Am      Dm    | F      G    | F            | F           |
          Oh…
        | Am      Dm    | F      G    | F            | F           |
          Oh…
```

Verse 3

```
         Am          Dm    Em
         But when she calls me,
            Am   G5    Am     G
         I do not walk, I run
              Am     Dm   Em
         Oh, when she calls, I
         Am    G5            Am    G
         Do not walk, I run.
        | Em           | C           | Am      G5   | Am      G   |
          Oh…
        | Em           | C           | B♭           | C           |
          Oh…
        | Am     Dm    | F      G    | F            | F           |
          Oh...
        | Am     Dm    | F      G    | F            | F           |
          Oh…
```

Coda

```
        | Am     Dm    | F      G    | F            | F           |
          Oh...
        | Am     Dm    | F      G    | F            | F           |
          Oh…
        | E♭           | E♭          | Am           ||
```

Work Is A Four Letter Word

Words by Don Black
Music by Guy Woolfenden

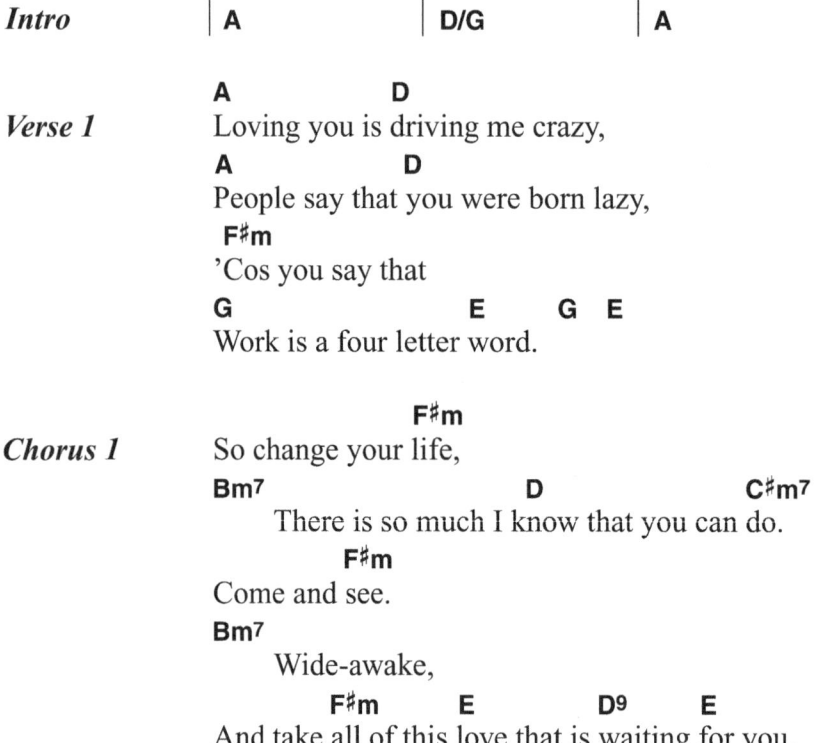

Capo second fret

Intro | A | D/G | A | D/G ‖

Verse 1
    A   D
Loving you is driving me crazy,
  A   D
People say that you were born lazy,
  F♯m
'Cos you say that
G   E   G E
Work is a four letter word.

Chorus 1
            F♯m
So change your life,
Bm7   D   C♯m7
   There is so much I know that you can do.
           F♯m
Come and see.
Bm7
   Wide-awake,
      F♯m   E   D9   E
And take all of this love that is waiting for you.

© Copyright 1987 Leeds Music Limited.
Universal/MCA Music Limited.
All Rights Reserved. International Copyright Secured.

Chorus 1 (cont.)

    A
If you stay,
    D
I'll stay right beside you.
    A
And my love,
    D
May help to remind you
  F#m   G   E   G E
To forget that work is a four letter word.

Verse 2

  A
I don't need
  D
A house that's a showplace,
  A
I just feel
  D
That we're going no place.
  F#m   G   E   G E
While you say that work is a four letter word.

Chorus 2   As Chorus 1

Verse 3   As Verse 2

Chorus 3

            F#m
So change your life,
Bm7   D   C#m7
    There is so much I know that you can do.
        F#m
Come and see.
Bm7
Wide-awake,
     F#m   E   D9   E
And take all of this love that is waiting for you.

Coda   ‖: E | E | E | E   :‖

Repeat to fade

You Just Haven't Earned It Yet, Baby

Words & Music by
Morrissey & Johnny Marr

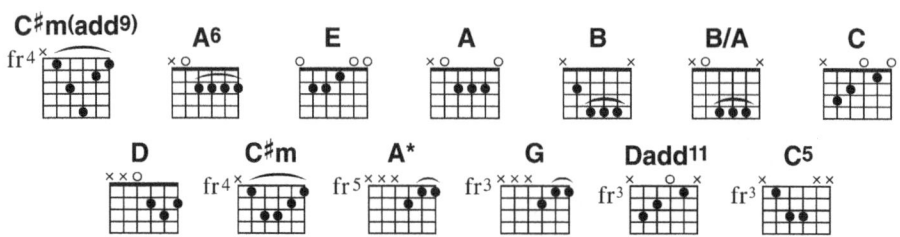

Capo second fret

Intro | C#m(add9) | A6 | E | E   A ||

Verse 1
      (A)   B   B/A   B   B/A
If you're wondering why
        B   B/A   B   B/A
All the love that you long for eludes you,
        B   B/A   B   B/A
And people are rude and cruel to you,
    E   A
I'll tell you why.
   B   B/A
I'll tell you why,
   B   B/A
I'll tell you why,
    B   B/A
I'll tell you why.

Bridge | E | C   D ||

© Copyright 1987 Marr Songs Limited/Artane Music Incorporated.
Chrysalis Music Limited (50%)/Universal Music Publishing Limited (50%).
All Rights Reserved. International Copyright Secured.

Chorus 1

     C♯m   A
You just haven't earned it yet, baby,
     E   B
You just haven't earned it, son.
     C♯m   A
You just haven't earned it yet, baby,
         E   B
You must suffer and cry for a longer time.
     C♯m   A
You just haven't earned it yet, baby,
    E
And I'm telling you now.

Verse 2

          B   B/A
If you're wondering why,
    B   B/A B   B/A   B   B/A
  When all I   wanted from life was to be famous,
     B   B/A   B   B/A
I have tried for so long, it's all gone wrong.
E   A
I'll tell you why,
B   B/A
   I'll tell you why,
B   B/A
   I'll tell you why,
    B   B/A
I'll tell you why.
E
   But you wouldn't believe me.

Chorus 2   As Chorus 1

Instrumental 1 ‖: B   B/A | B   B/A | B   B/A | B   B/A   :‖

	E A
Verse 3	I'll tell you why,
	B B/A
	I'll tell you why,
	B B/A
	Today I am remembering the time
	E
	When they pulled me back,
	And held me down,
	And looked me in the eyes and said…

	C♯m A
Chorus 3	"You just haven't earned it yet, baby,
	E B
	You just haven't earned it, my son.
	C♯m A
	You just haven't earned it yet, baby,
	E B
	You must stay on your own for slightly longer.
	C♯m A
	You just haven't earned it yet, baby,
	E
	And I'm telling you now…"

Instrumental 2 | A*   G | C   Dadd11 | A*   G | C   Dadd11 |
| B | B   C5   ‖

	(C5) C♯m A
Coda	"You just haven't earned it yet, baby.
	E B
	Oh, oh,
	C♯m A
	You just haven't earned it yet, baby
	E B
	Oh, oh."

‖: C♯m | A | E | B   C5 :‖

Repeat to fade

You've Got Everything Now

Words & Music by
Morrissey & Johnny Marr

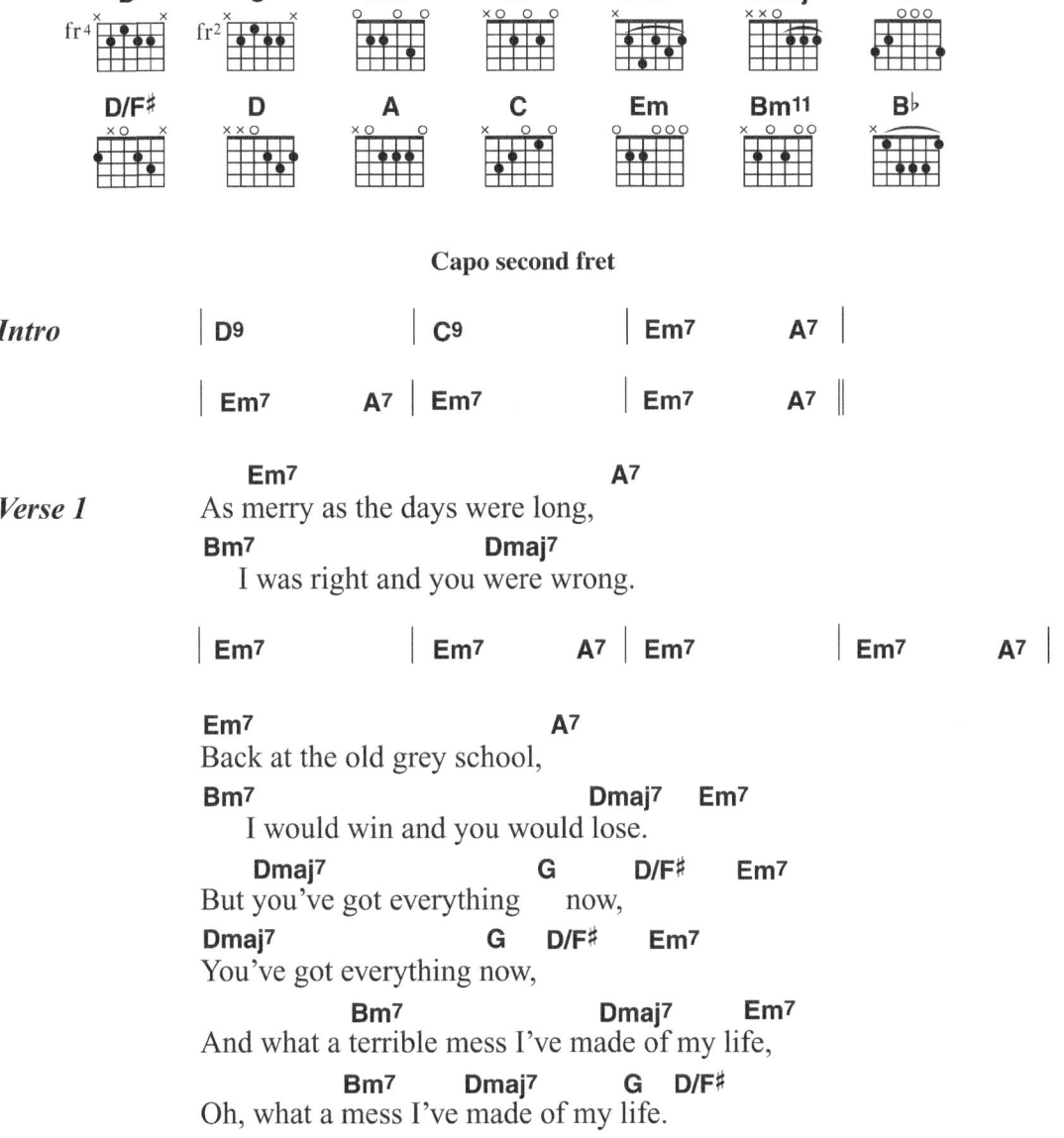

Capo second fret

Intro | D9 | C9 | Em7   A7 |
         | Em7   A7 | Em7 | Em7   A7 ||

Verse 1
    Em7   A7
As merry as the days were long,
 Bm7   Dmaj7
  I was right and you were wrong.

| Em7 | Em7   A7 | Em7 | Em7   A7 |

 Em7   A7
Back at the old grey school,
 Bm7   Dmaj7 Em7
  I would win and you would lose.
   Dmaj7   G   D/F# Em7
But you've got everything   now,
 Dmaj7   G   D/F# Em7
You've got everything now,
        Bm7   Dmaj7 Em7
And what a terrible mess I've made of my life,
     Bm7   Dmaj7 G D/F#
Oh, what a mess I've made of my life.

© Copyright 1984 Marr Songs Limited/Artane Music Incorporated.
Chrysalis Music Limited (50%)/Universal Music Publishing Limited (50%).
All Rights Reserved. International Copyright Secured.

Chorus 1

```
      D         A        G
      No, I've never had a job,
      A    Em
Because I've never wanted one.
        D/F#  G
I've seen you smile,
           A7              (D)
But I've never heard you laugh.
```

| D | C | D   A | G   A |

```
     A     Em                        D/F#  G    A7
     So who is rich and who is poor? I cannot say. Oh.
```

| D | C | D   A | G   A Em |

```
(Em)
Oh, you are your mother's only son,
    D/F#      G            A7
And you're a desperate one.
```

| D | C | D   A | |

```
G    A         Em
     But I don't want a lover,
                 D/F#      G      A7
I just want to be seen_____
```

| D | C | Bm11 | Bm11 | |

```
             Em7     A7
In the back of your car.
```

Verse 2

```
      Em7            A7
      A friendship sadly lost?
Bm7              Dmaj7
      Well, this is true and yet, it's false.
```

| Em7 | Em7   A7 | Em7 | Em7 | A7 |

```
             Em7    A7   Em7   A7
But did I ever tell you, by the way,
   Bm7          Dmaj7   Em7
   I never did like your face.
```

Verse 2 (cont.)

```
       Dmaj7          G  D/F#   Em7
But you've got everything    now,
       Dmaj7          G  D/F#   Em7
You've got everything now,
          Bm7              Dmaj7    Em7
And what a terrible mess I've made of my life,
          Bm7       Dmaj7      G   D/F#
Oh, what a mess I've made of my life.
```

Chorus 2

```
    D         A     G
   No, I've never had a job,
    A     Em
Because I'm too shy.
       D/F#  G
I've seen you smile,
       A7              (D)
But I've never heard you laugh.

| D           | C           | D      A    | G       A    |

    A     Em                        D/F#  G   A7
So who is rich and who is poor? I cannot say. Oh.

| D           | C           | D      A    | G       A  Em|

Em
Oh, you are your mother's only son,
   D/F#      G            A7
And you're a desperate one.

| D           | C           | D      A    |

G    A         Em
  But I don't want a lover,
               D/F#       G      A7
I just want to be tied_____
```

Coda

```
||: D         | C           | G           | Bb      C    |
                              In the back of         your____

   | D         | C           | G           | Bb      C   :||
   car.
```

Repeat ad lib. to fade

THE SMITHS
DISCOGRAPHY

DATE	TITLE	LABEL/ CAT. NO.	U.K. CHART POSITION

7-Inch Singles

1983
May	Hand In Glove/Handsome Devil	RT 131	
Nov	This Charming Man/Jeane	RT 136	25

A limited number of test pressings of the cancelled 'Reel Around The Fountain'/'Jeane' are in existence

1984
Jan	What Difference Does It Make?/Back To The Old House	RT 146	12
May	Heaven Knows I'm Miserable Now/Suffer Little Children	RT 156	19
Aug	William, It Was Really Nothing/Please, Please, Please, Let Me Get What I Want	RT 166	17

During February 1984 a limited number of DJ-only promotional copies of 'Still Ill'/'You've Got Everything Now' (R61 DJ) were circulated in order to plug the group's debut album

1985
Feb	How Soon Is Now?/Well I Wonder	RT 176	24
Mar	Shakespeare's Sister/What She Said	RT 181	26
July	That Joke Isn't Funny Anymore/Meat Is Murder (Live)	RT 186	49
Sept	The Boy With The Thorn In His Side/Asleep	RT 191	23

1986
May	Bigmouth Strikes Again/Money Changes Everything	RT 192	26
July	Panic/Vicar In A Tutu	RT 193	11
Oct	Ask/Cemetry Gates	RT 194	14

1987
Jan	Shoplifters Of The World Unite/Half A Person	RT 195	12
Apr	Sheila Take A Bow/Is It Really So Strange?	RT 196	10
July	Girlfriend In A Coma/Work Is A Four Letter Word	RT 197	13
Oct	I Started Something I Couldn't Finish/Pretty Girls Makes Graves	RT 198	23
Dec	Last Night I Dreamt That Somebody Loved Me/Rusholme Ruffians	RT 200	30

DATE	TITLE	LABEL/ CAT. NO.	U.K. CHART POSITION
1992			
Aug	This Charming Man/Jeane	WEA YZ 0001	8
Sept	How Soon Is Now?/Hand In Glove	WEA YZ 0002	16
Dec	There Is A Light That Never Goes Out/ Hand In Glove (Live)	WEA YZ 0003	25

DATE	TITLE	LABEL/CAT. NO.

12-Inch Singles/CD Singles

DATE	TITLE	LABEL/CAT. NO.
1983		
Nov	This Charming Man (Manchester)/ This Charming Man (London)/ Accept Yourself/Wonderful Woman	RTT 136
Dec	This Charming Man (New York Mix – Vocal)/ This Charming Man (New York Mix – Instrumental)	RT 136
1984		
Feb	What Difference Does It Make?/ Back To The Old House/These Things Take Time	RTT 146
May	Heaven Knows I'm Miserable Now/ Suffer Little Children/Girl Afraid	RTT 156
Aug	William, It Was Really Nothing/Please, Please, Please, Let Me Get What I Want/How Soon Is Now?	RTT 166
1985		
Jan	Barbarism Begins At Home/Barbarism Begins At Home *(A promotion only release in a limited edition of 500 copies)*	RTT 171
Feb	How Soon Is Now?/Well I Wonder/Oscillate Wildly	RTT 176
Mar	Shakespeare's Sister/What She Said/Stretch Out And Wait	RTT 181
July	That Joke Isn't Funny Anymore/Nowhere Fast (Live)/ Stretch Out And Wait (Live)/Shakespeare's Sister (Live)/ Meat Is Murder (Live)	RTT 186
Sept	The Boy With The Thorn In His Side/Asleep/Rubber Ring	RTT 191
1986		
May	Bigmouth Strikes Again/Money Changes Everything/ Unloveable	RTT 192

DATE	TITLE	LABEL/CAT. NO.
July	Panic/Vicar In A Tutu/The Draize Train	RTT 193
Oct	Ask/Cemetry Gates/Golden Lights	RTT 194

1987

Jan	Shoplifters Of The World Unite/Half A Person/London *(Initial versions of 'Shoplifters Of The World Unite' were despatched with 'You Just Haven't Earned It Yet, Baby' on the A-side)*	RTT 195
April	Sheila Take A Bow/Is It Really So Strange?/ Sweet And Tender Hooligan	RTT 196
July	Girlfriend In A Coma/Work Is A Four Letter Word/ I Keep Mine Hidden	RTT 197
Oct	I Started Something I Couldn't Finish/Pretty Girls Make Graves/ Some Girls Are Bigger Than Others *(Cassette versions of the single included a cover version of James' 'What's The World?', recorded live in Glasgow)*	RT 198
Dec	Last Night I Dreamt That Somebody Loved Me/ Rusholme Ruffians/Nowhere Fast *(The CD version of this single featured an extra track: 'William, It Was Really Nothing')*	RTT 200

1988

Nov	Barbarism Begins At Home/Shakespeare's Sister/ Stretch Out And Wait	RTT 171 CD
Nov	The Headmaster Ritual/Nowhere Fast (Live)/ Stretch Out And Wait (Live)/Meat Is Murder (Live)	RTT 215 CD

1992

Aug	This Charming Man/Wonderful Woman/Accept Yourself	
Aug	This Charming Man (Manchester Mix)/ Jeane/Wonderful Woman/Accept Yourself	YZ0001CD1
Aug	This Charming Man (Manchester Mix)/This Charming Man (London Mix)/This Charming Man (New York Mix)/ This Charming Man (New York Instrumental)/ This Charming Man (Peel Session)/This Charming Man (Single Remix)/ This Charming Man (Original Single Version)	YZ0001CD2
Sept	How Soon Is Now? (Edit)/The Queen Is Dead/Handsome Devil/ I Started Something I Couldn't Finish	YZ0002CD1
Sept	I Know It's Over/Suffer Little Children/Back To The Old House/ How Soon Is Now? (Album Version)	YZ0002CD2
Dec	There Is A Light That Never Goes Out/Hand In Glove (Live)/ Some Girls Are Bigger Than Others (Live)/Money Changes Everything	YZ0003CD1

DATE	TITLE	LABEL/CAT. NO.
Dec	There Is A Light That Never Goes Out/Hand In Glove (featuring Sandie Shaw)/I Don't Owe You Anything (featuring Sandie Shaw)/Jeane (featuring Sandie Shaw)	YZ0003CD2

In addition to the above, The Smiths have appeared on various samplers, imports and rare special promotion discs and test pressings. Rough Trade retrospectively issued several of The Smiths' 12-inch singles on CD. Strangely, the transference from vinyl to CD single was never completed and the ordering of releases was not chronological. Those back catalogue singles that did emerge on Rough Trade CD included 'What Difference Does It Make?', 'Williams, It Was Really Nothing', 'The Boy With The Thorn In His Side', 'Panic', 'Ask' and 'Last Night I Dreamt That Somebody Loved Me'. Catalogue numbers were the same as the Rough Trade 12-inch releases, with the suffix "CD".

DATE	TITLE	LABEL/CAT. NO.	U.K. CHART POSITION

Albums

1984

Feb	**The Smiths** Reel Around The Fountain; You've Got Everything Now; Miserable Lie; Pretty Girls Make Graves; The Hand That Rocks The Cradle; Still Ill; Hand In Glove; What Difference Does It Make?; I Don't Owe You Anything; Suffer Little Children. *CD edition (Rough CD61) released Oct 1986*	Rough 61	2
Nov	**Hatful Of Hollow** William, It Was Really Nothing; What Different Does It Make?; These Things Take Time; This Charming Man; How Soon Is Now?; Handsome Devil; Hand In Glove; Still Ill; Heaven Knows I'm Miserable Now; This Night Has Opened My Eyes; You've Got Everything Now; Accept Yourself; Girl Afraid; Back To The Old House; Reel Around The Fountain; Please, Please, Please, Let Me Get I Want. *CD edition (Rough CD76) released Dec 1985*	Rough 76	7

1985

Feb	**Meat Is Murder** The Headmaster Ritual; Rusholme Ruffians; I Want The One I Can't Have; What She Said; That Joke Isn't Funny Anymore; Nowhere Fast, Well I Wonder, Barbarism Begins At Home; Meat Is Murder. *CD edition (Rough CD81) released Apr 1985*	Rough 81	1

1986

June	**The Queen Is Dead** The Queen Is Dead; Frankly, Mr Shankly; I Know It's Over; Never Had No One Ever; Cemetry Gates; Bigmouth Strikes Again; The Boy With The Thorn In His Side; Vicar In A Tutu; There Is A Light That Never Goes Out; Some Girls Are Bigger Than Others. *CD edition (Rough CD96) released June 1986*	Rough 96	2

DATE	TITLE	LABEL/ CAT. NO.	U.K. CHART POSITION

1987

Mar   **The World Won't Listen**   Rough 101   2
Panic; Ask; London; Bigmouth Strikes Again;
Shakespeare's Sister; There Is A Light That Never Goes Out;
Shoplifters Of The World Unite; The Boy With The Thorn
In His Side; Asleep; Unloveable; Half A Person; Stretch Out
And Wait; That Joke Isn't Funny Anymore; Oscillate Wildly;
You Just Haven't Earned It Yet, Baby; Rubber Ring.
CD edition (Rough CD101) released Mar 1987

Apr   **Louder Than Bombs**   Rough 255/Sire 9 25569-1   38
Is It Really So Strange?; Shelia Take A Bow;
Shoplifters Of The World Unite; Sweet And Tender Hooligan;
Half A Person; London; Panic; Girl Afraid; Shakespeare's Sister;
William, It Was Really Nothing; You Just Haven't Earned It Yet, Baby;
Heaven Knows I'm Miserable Now; Ask; Golden Lights; Oscillate Wildly;
These Things Take Time; Rubber Ring; Back To The Old House;
Hand In Glove; Stretch Out And Wait; Please, Please, Please, Let
Me Get I Want; This Night Has Opened My Eyes; Unloveable; Asleep.
CD edition (Sire CD 9 25569-2) released Apr 1987

Sept   **Strangeways, Here We Come**   Rough 106   2
A Rush And A Push And The Land Is Ours; I Started
Something I Couldn't Finish; Death Of A Disco Dancer;
Girlfriend In A Coma; Stop Me If You Think You've Heard
This One Before; Last Night I Dreamt That Somebody Loved Me;
Unhappy Birthday; Paint A Vulgar Picture; Death At One's Elbow;
I Won't Share You.
CD edition (Rough CD106) released Sept 1987

1988

Sept   **Rank**   Rough 126   2
The Queen Is Dead; Panic; Vicar In A Tutu; Ask;
Rusholme Ruffians/(Marie's The Name) His Latest Fame (Medley);
The Boy With The Thorn In His Side; What She Said; Is It Really
So Strange?; Cemetry Gates; London; I Know It's Over;
The Draize Train; Still Ill; Bigmouth Strikes Again.
CD edition (Rough CD126) released Sept 1988

Oct   **The Peel Sessions**   Strange Fruit SF PS 055   -
What Difference Does It Make?; Miserable Lie;
Reel Around The Fountain; Handsome Devil.
CD edition (SF PS CD 055) released Oct 1988